GW00494235

Cecilia Norman

The Gourmet Guide to Instant Preserves

JAMS & PICKLES
IN THE MICROWAVE

First published in 1991 by Absolute Press,
14 Widcombe Crescent, Bath BA2 6AH, England.

The right of Cecilia Norman to be identified as author of this
work has been asserted by her in accordance with the Copyright,
Designs and Patents Act 1988.

Design: Monica Chia
Illustrations: Jane Hughes
Photoset and printed by The Longdunn Press Ltd, Bristol

ISBN 0 948230 44 4

Contents

Introduction

Preserving using the microwave is a joy – it is fast, it is clean and it needs very little attention. True colour is maintained due to the short cooking times. **The only basic equipment needed is a large oven – glass bowl, wooden spoon, strainer, and jars and jam pot covers.** When using conventional methods constant stirring is required to prevent burning which occurs as a result of the direct contact between the base of the pan and the hob. This cannot happen in the microwave since there is no direct heat. Nothing is more demoralising than having to face up to burnt preserves **and** a burnt pan.

It is fun and great pleasure to make preserves on an impulse. When the first summer berries appear on the bushes, no matter how few, you can still make enough fresh jam to titillate the most jaded palate. You can afford to be tempted by the plethora of fruit on the greengrocer's stall, buying just enough for 'jam for tea' or a little bit extra to make preserves that will store in the refrigerator for a week or two.

Fruit jellies are equally easy to make and the only additional ingredient need be sugar. Fruit cheeses, curds and butters are quick to prepare and when no fresh fruit is available frozen or long-life juices are good substitutes.

My favourite is Fresh Strawberry Preserve with extra just-ripe berries cut up and added towards the end of cooking, and my easy Ruby Orange and Grapefruit Marmalade microwaves the fruit whole for easy handling. The pulp and pips come away like a dream and shredding the cooked peel is simple. Just imagine Jamaican

Conserve with chopped crunchy pineapple, chopped sultanas and rum, Damson, Madeira and Almond Jelly, Blueberry and Cassis Fruit Curd and Sparkling Lemon Curd with added chopped lemon to give a sharp/sweet flavour and contrasting textures.

Whole fruit preserving is almost effortless. Try Preserved Kumquats, the syrup picks up the orangey flavour which develops on keeping. Whiskey Tipple Apricots probably should not be eaten just before driving but Pitted Cherries in Honey Syrup won't cause inebriation. Chapter 5 has only a handful of recipes because Candied Fruit is more time-consuming, but do try them out and then vary the fruit, peel and nuts to increase your recipe repertoire of special occasion goodies.

Nowadays bottling has become a less popular form of preservation. Vegetable bottling was never highly recommended because of the dangers of food poisoning and in any case there seems little purpose when modern times have provided us with freezers which are a far more reliable method of storage. In general, fruit bottling is not advised in the microwave oven. The use of metal clips could be disastrous but the microwave can be used in several ways to hasten the process and syrups of varying strengths can be simply and speedily produced for all uses.

No book on preserves would be complete without the inclusion of savoury jellies to enhance cold meats, fish and poultry as well as bringing vegetarian dishes into the luxury class. Here you will find instructions for Clear Bergamot and other unusual jellies.

Piccalilli, Tomato and Capsicum chutneys are among the recipes in the pickle and chutney section and some interesting ketchups and vinegars are to be found in the final section of the book.

I am sure you will find preserving using the microwave as fascinating as I do and I hope that you will find this book helpful.

Covering

Throughout the recipes the methods include instructions "cook covered or uncovered". Although cling-film is a permissible covering if it does not touch the food I prefer to use a microwaveable lid. These are easily obtained from microwave accessory stockists or mail order from Lakeland Plastics. The one-size lid fits over or into most bowls and is fitted with a vent to minimise boiling over. Cling-film must be vented – to do this pull back one corner to leave a gap. Alternatively suitable dinner plates can be used as a cover, but are difficult to balance should venting be necessary. As the heat builds up in the preserves, the bowls become too hot to handle and it is essential to use oven-gloves when taking them in and out of the microwave oven.

Bowls

The bowls used in the preparation of recipes for this book were Pyrex, although other high temperature resistant makes may be used. Check with the manufacturer's instructions before embarking on high sugar content cookery.

Bowl sizes

The medium bowl has a 1.1 litre/2 pint capacity
The large bowl has a 2 litre/3½ pint capacity
The very large bowl has a 2.8 litre/5 pint capacity

Other measures

The spoons used are all level and conform to the British Standard:–
$$1.25ml = ¼ \text{ teaspoon}$$
$$2.5ml = ½ \text{ teaspoon}$$
$$5ml = 1 \text{ teaspoon}$$
$$15ml = 1 \text{ tablespoon}$$

It should be noted that Imperial and metric measures are not interchangeable in any one recipe.

While the author has taken every care to ensure the success of the recipes she can accept no responsibility in the event of mishaps.

GUIDE TO PECTIN AND ACID IN FRUIT

FRUIT	PECTIN	ACID
Apples	High	Medium
Apricots	Medium	Medium
Blackberries	Medium	Medium
Blackcurrants	High	High
Blueberries	Medium	Medium
Cherries	Low	Medium
Clementines	High	Medium
Crab apples	High	Medium
Cranberries	High	Medium
Damsons	High	High
Elderberries	Low	Low
Figs	Low	Low
Gooseberries	High	High
Grapefruit	High	High
Grapes	Medium	Medium
Greengages	Medium	High
Kiwi fruit	Low	Low
Lemons	High	High
Limes	High	High
Loganberries	Medium	Medium
Mangoes	Low	Low
Melons	Low	Low
Nectarines	Low	Low
Oranges	High	Medium
Peaches	Low	Low
Pears	Low	Low
Pineapples	Low	Medium

8

Plums	High	High
Quinces (unripe)	High	Low
Raspberries	Medium	Medium
Redcurrants	High	High
Rhubarb	Low	High
Sloes	High	High
Starfruit (Carambolas)	Medium	High
Strawberries	Low	Low
Tangerines	Medium	Medium

The Recipes

1 Jams, Marmalades, Preserves and Conserves

Blackcurrant and Redcurrant Jam
Carrot and Pistachio Marmalade
Cheater's Jam
Fresh Strawberry Preserve
Jamaican Pineapple Conserve
Pecan and Damson Jam
Rhubarb, Grapefuit and Stem Ginger Jam
Ruby Orange and Grapefruit Marmalade
Starfruit, Lime and Red Pear Jam
Weekend Blackberry and Apple Jam

2 Fruit Jellies

Apple Jelly
Apple Pectin
Damson, Madeira and Almond Jelly
Loganberry Jelly
Mocha and Lime Jelly
Pure Grapefruit Jelly
Strawberry and Redcurrant Jelly

10

3 Curds and Fruit Cheeses

Apple Butter
Apricot and Orange Spread
Blueberry and Cassis Fruit Curd
Damson and Grape Cheese
Gooseberry and Kiwi Curd
Nectarine Cheese
Raspberry Curd
Reduced Sugar Lime Curd
Sparkling Lemon Curd

4 Whole Preserved Fruit and Spiced Fruit

Cardamom Spiced Oranges
Figs in Brandy
Honeyed Greengages
Pineapple in Curaçao
Pitted Cherries in Honey Syrup
Preserved Kumquats
Sweet and Sour Ginger Peaches
Whiskey Tipple Apricots

5 Candied and Crystallized Fruit

Candied Grapes
Candied Peel
Marrons Glacés
Sugared Walnuts

6 Syrups

Blackthorn Syrup
Lemon Cordial

Lemon Sorbet
Raspberry and Orange Syrup
Sorbet Syrup
Stock Syrup
Strawberry Cointreau Sorbet
Syrups for Bottling

7 Savoury Jellies

Celery Leaf Jelly
Clear Bergamot Jelly
Clementine and Mint Jelly
Grape and Cinnamon Jelly
Parsley and Marjoram Jelly
Quince and Lemon Balm Jelly
Redcurrant Jelly

8 Pickles, Chutneys and Relishes

Beetroot and Horseradish Relish
Green Banana Chutney
Lemon Tomato Chutney
Mango Chutney
Piccalilli
Pickled Red Cabbage
Ploughman's Chutney
Sweetcorn Relish
Tomato and Capsicum Chutney

9 Ketchups, Barbecue Sauces and Vinegars

Elderberry Ketchup
Hot and Peppery Barbecue Sauce
Impromptu Barbecue Sauce

Lemon and Orange Enhancer Sauce
Lemon Verbena Marinade
Natural Tomato Ketchup
Raspberry Vinegar
Spiced Vinegar
Victoria Catchup

CHAPTER ONE

Jams, Marmalades, Preserves and Conserves

Delicious jams result from the combination of good quality fruit, the correct amount of pectin, acid, sugar, liquid and, of course, cooking times. Each of the recipes in this chapter has been designed to create the right balance and produce a jam to be proud of. No added preservatives or artificial colourings have been introduced so that shelf-life is necessarily reduced. The basic concept of this book is to obtain the best possible quality with the minimum cooking time so as to retain a true clear colour. In some instances the set will be less firm and more like the consistency of the jams found in France.

Anyone finding the title of this chapter confusing may be interested in the following definitions:

A jam is a thick combination of fruit or vegetables with sugar in which most or all of the fruit is crushed but may contain some larger pieces.
A conserve contains sharper fruit and is usually made up of two main ingredients, one of them being dried fruit, nuts or citrus.
A preserve in this context has a slacker consistency.

THE BASICS

Generally speaking, the fruit should be only just ripe. Over-ripe fruit is short on pectin.

Pectin is the starchy cellulose substance that creates the 'gel' and fundamentally comes from cooking apples, redcurrants, blackcurrants, gooseberries or plums. Plum pectin is sometimes used commercially but for domestic use, apple pectin is probably the most suitable as neither the flavour nor the colour is overpowering. A recipe for apple pectin is on page 34. Alternatively pectin can be introduced with commercially manufactured bottled pectin eg Certo. This is suitable to use in jams containing pronounced flavoured fruit. Bottled pectins also deepen the colour. Kept in cool conditions a bottle of pectin is a useful item to have at hand. It can be added at the end of cooking to

16

improve the 'set'. **Jam sugar** or **Sugar with Pectin** also contains an acid such as tartaric. Used in place of granulated or preserving sugar their advantage is that cooking times after reaching boiling point are reduced. You may need to increase the weight of jam sugar when substituting for pure sugar, as the added pectin counts for part of the sugar's weight.

Acid

To improve the 'gel' in low acid fruits and improve the colour and prevent crystallization, most jams must have additional acid. This can be in the form of lemon juice, citric acid, tartaric acid or apple pectin. 450g/1pound fruit requires 2 teaspoons fresh lemon juice, 1/2 teaspoon citric or tartaric acid crystals or 3 tablespoons apple pectin.

Sugar

White sugar is preferable to demerara as it adds no additional colour. Preserving sugar has larger crystals and gives the truest colour but I find granulated is a good all-rounder. Jam sugar has been described previously. Apart from the low sugar jams which possess a looser set and have poorer keeping qualities, it is not a good idea to reduce sugar ratios. In the recipes I have chosen the type of sugar which I found gave the best results.

Cooking Times

Unlike the conventional method, the degree of cooking or 'doneness' is governed by several different factors. Cold ingredients take longer than those at room temperature; larger quantities longer than small; the weight of sugar; the volume of water; whether the bowl is or is not covered; the diameter of the bowl and the power of the microwave oven. This last element is the vital one and is more important than all the others. The higher the power the better the

17

likely success. Low powered ovens do not reach the level required to maintain an adequate fast boil. Some models, notably older ones which have become tired, may not be running at their rated power. Also if the microwave has been in continuous use for a lengthy period, say an hour, its efficiency is temporarily diminished. The solutions to these problems are to reduce the quantity of liquid on low rated or aged machines, or increase the sugar content. Allow a period of time to elapse for the microwave to recover its strength, then cook for a further period. Add liquid pectin or thicken with gelatine. New microwave ovens will soon have to conform to standards which require them to perform to a given wattage rating. But do bear in mind that no two ovens work synonymously as indeed no two identical cars give exactly the same performance.

I have endeavoured to give sound guidelines and timings and have erred on the safe side. You may find that you have to adjust your cooking times depending on the various contributory factors. Conventional preserving is much more hazardous than doing it by microwave and all that stirring and burning is enough to put off all except the doughty jam maker.

The Sequence

1 Read the recipe through to the end.
2 Get out the utensils including the recommended size bowl.
3 Prepare and cook the fruit to release the pectin.
4 Do the pectin test if you wish.
5 Make sure the sugar is completely dissolved before boiling.
6 Test for setting. Microwave jams continue cooking for a few seconds after the power is switched off.
7 Continue cooking if necessary.
8 Prepare the jars if the jam is going to be stored for more than a day or two.
9 Pot.

The Pectin Test

Before adding the sugar put *one* teaspoon of the fruit juice in a small narrow glass. Leave for a minute to cool.
Add 3 teaspoons methylated spirits. Swirl gently for 15 seconds.
If a soft but whole jelly-like clot forms, the pectin content is high.
Two or three separate clots indicate a medium content.
When the clot breaks easily into several small lumps the juice has very little or no pectin. DO NOT TASTE.
Cook the fruit for a few more minutes then retest.
Remember to add pectin at the appropriate time allowing 3 fluid ounces to each 450g/ 1 pound of fruit.
After testing, throw away the methylated spirit mixture and wash the glass thoroughly in detergent.

The setting tests

The wrinkle test which is most often recommended is the most reliable. A few drops of the jam liquid placed on a chilled saucer should wrinkle when pushed with a spoon.

In the flake test mentioned in some recipes a few drops of the freshly cooked jam are lifted above the bowl, held for a few seconds to allow the liquid to cool, then turned sideways. Most of the liquid will drip into the bowl leaving a last recalcitrant drop hanging like a pearl from the edge of the spoon, a sharp shake being required to release it.

Thermometer tests are not highly satisfactory in microwaved jam.

Preparing the jars

· Use clean jam jars. Add water to a depth of 2.5cm/ 1 inch.
· Place in the microwave and heat on Full power for 30 seconds or until boiling.
· Using oven gloves carefully remove the jar(s), swirl the water around, then empty out. Shake out any surplus drips.

Potting

There is no need to pot the jam unless you wish to store it.

Pour or ladle the jam into the hot jars. Using a wide-mouthed funnel or jug will avoid getting jam running down the outside of the jars. If needed, wipe the rim with a hot wet cloth. Fill to within 6mm/ ¼ inch of the rim. Place a small waxed disc directly on to the jam. Moisten one side of the cellophane circle and place wet-side uppermost on the jar. Secure with the elastic band. Jam pot cover kits are readily available in stationers or hardware shops.

When the jam is cool keep it in the refrigerator. Some preserves will keep for ages in the freezer but they are best stored in freezer containers.

Marmalades present no problems in the microwave oven, the main thing being that the peel has to be completely cooked before being added to the sugar. Peel can become unpalatably tough if mixed with the sugar too soon. Conventional recipes can sometimes be adapted, but this is not invariably so. It is however safe to adapt the citrus recipe in this chapter, varying the fruit while making sure of the total weight equivalent. Using the very large bowl it is possible to achieve a yield of up to 2.25kg/ 5 pounds. Increase the cooking times accordingly.

Although doubling up the ingredients is possible, a longer cooking period darkens the preserve. A double quantity will not necessarily take double the time at each stage and overall probably only takes half as much again.

Soft Berries such as blackberries, raspberries, strawberries and loganberries are by far the easiest to cook. Add 225g/ 8 ounces of granulated sugar to each 225g/ 8 ounces of berries – it doesn't matter whether the berries are fresh or frozen. Stir until all the sugar is moist and coloured. Without covering heat on Full power for about 4 minutes. Stir the mixture gently until all the sugar is dissolved, then cook uncovered on Full power until there is a slight wrinkling of the syrup (about 7 minutes). Do not expect a very firm set but the jam sets quite firmly upon cooling.

Berries in skins such as blackcurrants, redcurrants and gooseberries must be cooked in a little water before the sugar is added. If not the skins will become very tough. Put the fruit in a large bowl with a few tablespoons of water, three-quarters cover and cook, stirring occasionally, for about 7 minutes until the fruit softens. Uncover and stir in the sugar until it has dissolved, which will happen quickly since the fruit is hot. Without further covering cook on Full power for about 12 minutes depending on the quantity until setting point is reached.

Plum and greengage jam require no additional water and a little less cooking than the tougher-skinned berries. Use the same proportions of sugar to fruit and you can use up to 900g/ 2 pounds of each. Cooking will take approximately half as long again.

Low Sugar Jams do not set very well and must be consumed in a very short time. Dieters will be pleased to know that these jams are lower in calories but they will not be suitable for Diabetics. Choose fruit with a high pectin and acid content to assist the 'gel'. Sugar substitutes such as saccharine cannot be substituted for sugar but fructose used in a lesser proportion than sucrose has considerable sweetening properties and a set can be achieved by thickening with gelatine, agar-agar or arrowroot. Provided that the weight of fructose together with the sugar contained in the fruit itself is acceptable to the patient's diet, the diabetic may be allowed a scraping of preserves made in this way. No specific recipes are contained in the book.

BLACKCURRANT AND REDCURRANT JAM

100g/ 4 ounces redcurrants, weighed after trimming
225g/ 8 ounces blackcurrants, weighed after trimming
350g/ 12 ounces granulated sugar

Put the fruit and 200ml/ 7 fl.oz water in a very large bowl, cover and cook on Full power for about 7 minutes or until the fruit softens. Stir occasionally to prevent boiling over.
Add the sugar, mixing until nearly dissolved. Without covering, cook on Full power for 2 minutes, then stir to completely dissolve the sugar. Continue cooking for 14 minutes or until a drop of the syrup hangs from the side of a spoon.
Pot in hot sterilised jars.

Makes about 675g/ 1½ pounds.

CARROT AND PISTACHIO MARMALADE

1 orange
1 lemon
225g/ 8 ounces carrots
25g/ 1 ounce shelled pistachio nuts
450g/ 1 pound granulated sugar

Grate the orange and lemon rind. Squeeze the juice from the lemon, remove pith and pips from the orange, then chop the flesh. Peel and grate the carrots. Finely chop the pistachios.
Mix all the ingredients including the sugar in a very large bowl. Cook on Full power for 2 minutes. Stir until the sugar is dissolved. Cook on Full power for about 5 minutes, then stir well. Continue cooking

for 12 minutes or until a little of the syrup spooned on to a chilled saucer wrinkles when pushed with a spoon handle.

Makes 450g/ 1 pound.

CHEATER'S JAM

2 × 400g/ 14 ounce cans apricots in natural juice
3 tablespoons lemon juice
550g/ 1¼ pounds jam sugar
small knob of butter

Purée the apricots, 225ml/ 8 fl.oz of their juice and the lemon juice. Pour into a very large bowl and stir in the sugar. Cover and cook on Full power for 5 minutes, then stir until the sugar is dissolved. Without covering cook on Full power for 5 minutes.
Stir in the butter and continue cooking for 15 minutes, stirring occasionally. Test for setting by placing a spoonful of the mixture on a chilled saucer. The jam should wrinkle when pushed with a spoon. Continue cooking for a further 5 minutes or until a satisfactory set is reached. Pot in the usual way.

Makes about 900g/ 2 pounds.

Vary this store cupboard recipe by substituting peaches, pears or other canned fruit and add a pinch of ground ginger, mace or cloves.

FRESH STRAWBERRY PRESERVE

450g / 1 pound fresh unblemished strawberries
350g / 12 ounces jam sugar
small knob of butter

Hull the strawberries and cut them into quarters.

Reserve 100g / 4 ounces of the fruit and put the remainder in a very large bowl with 1 tablespoon of water.

Cover and cook on Full power for 2 minutes, then gently fold in the sugar until no white crystals are visible. Cover and cook for 2 minutes. Stir carefully until the sugar is completely dissolved.

Uncover and continue cooking for 4 minutes, then stir in the butter to reduce foaming. Cook for a further 4 minutes or until a drop of the syrup hangs firmly from the spoon.

Stir in the remaining strawberries and continue cooking for 4 minutes. Re-test, then leave to cool.

It is essential to attain a firm set. Test before adding the reserved fruit as the additional juice provided loosens the mixture.

Makes about 675g / 1½ pounds.

JAMAICAN PINEAPPLE CONSERVE

50g / 2 ounces sultanas
1 small ripe pineapple
1 large lemon
225g / 8 ounces jam sugar
2 tablespoons dark Jamaican rum

Halve the sultanas and set aside. Before peeling the pineapple remove the top and bottom slices and place upright on a board over a tray (to catch the juice). Peel vertically with a sharp knife removing all the woody 'eyes'. Cut the pineapple into 4 wedges and remove the pithy centre if necessary. Weigh 225g / 8 ounces of the pineapple, then cut into small dice. Grate the lemon rind and squeeze the juice.

Mix the diced pineapple, the collected juice, the grated lemon rind and juice in a very large bowl.

Cover and cook on Full power for 2 minutes to soften the pineapple. Stir the sugar in thoroughly. Cook uncovered for 2 minutes, stir until sugar is completely dissolved, then continue cooking for 6 minutes or until a drop of the syrup hangs from a wooden spoon.

Stir in the sultanas and rum and cook for a further 3 minutes to enable the sultanas to swell. The mixture will still appear runny but the wrinkled surface indicates that the conserve will set upon cooling.

Makes 450g / 1 pound.

Use up any surplus pineapple in fruit salad.

PECAN AND DAMSON JAM

450g/ 1 pound damsons
550g/ 1¼ pounds granulated sugar
175g/ 6 ounces shelled pecan nuts

Put the damsons in a very large bowl with 175ml/ 6 fl.oz water. Cover and cook on Full power for 7 minutes or until the fruit is tender. Stir frequently during cooking. Using a fork or slotted spoon remove as many of the stones as possible.

Add the sugar and stir until completely dissolved. The heat of the fruit will make this happen more quickly.

Meanwhile put the nuts in a bowl, cover with cold water, put in the microwave and cook on Full power until boiling. Drain thoroughly (this process removes any bitterness from the nuts and is particularly necessary if the nuts are not fresh). Finely chop the nuts and set aside. Return the bowl of damsons to the microwave and without covering cook on Full power for 10 minutes. Stir in the nuts and continue cooking for 5 minutes or until a drop of the syrup hangs from a wooden spoon. Leave for a few minutes before potting. Should the nuts rise to the surface of the jam, stir before sealing.

Makes about 675g/ 1½ pounds.

Provided you have a freezer with a large capacity it is a good idea to freeze the fruit immediately after gathering for use in recipes such as this. Cook from the frozen state, allowing about 5 minutes extra initial cooking time.

RHUBARB, GRAPEFRUIT AND STEM GINGER JAM

225g/ 8 ounces rhubarb, weighed after trimming
2 walnut-sized pieces stem ginger
6 tablespoons grapefruit juice
225g/ 8 ounces jam sugar
2 tablespoons ginger syrup from the jar

Wipe the rhubarb and cut into 1cm/½ inch slices. Finely chop the stem ginger.

Put the rhubarb and grapefruit juice in a very large bowl. Cover with a vented lid or with cling film leaving a sizeable gap to prevent overspill. Cook on Full power stirring occasionally for 5 – 7 minutes or until the fruit is pulpy.

Stir in the sugar and the ginger syrup and cook for 2 minutes, then stir until the sugar is completely dissolved. Cook uncovered for 5 minutes or until setting point is reached. Mix in the chopped ginger. Leave to cool.

Makes 450g/ 1 pound.

RUBY ORANGE AND GRAPEFRUIT MARMALADE

2 blood oranges
1 pink grapefruit } total weight 800g/ 1¾ pounds
1 lemon
800g/ 1¾ pounds jam sugar

Wash and wipe the fruit, and pierce each in two or three places to prevent bursting. Put in a very large bowl with 300ml/ ½ pint boiling water. Cover with a lid or plate and cook on Full power for about 20 minutes or until the fruit is soft and the peel is tender. Turn the fruit over half-way through cooking. Sometimes one of the fruits will collapse during cooking but this is unimportant.

Using oven gloves remove the lid, then take the bowl out of the Microwave. Remove the fruit with a slotted spoon, then stir the sugar into the liquid left in the bowl. Cook on Full power for about 3 minutes, then stir until the sugar is dissolved.

Using a sharp knife and fork cut the fruit into quarters. Discard the pips. Very finely shred the oranges and lemon including the pith and attached pulp. Scrape off and reserve the grapefruit pulp, slice away and discard the pith, then finely shred the peel.

Mix the fruit pulp and peel into the syrupy liquid and without covering cook on Full power for 12 minutes, stirring once. Test for setting by dropping a spoon of the syrup on to a chilled saucer, leave for a few moments to cool, then push with the side of a spoon when the syrup should wrinkle.

Leave to cool slightly, then stir before potting in sterilised jars. Stirring will ensure that the peel and liquid are evenly mixed. Seal in the usual way.

Makes 1 – 1.5 kg/ 2¼ – 3 pounds.

STAR FRUIT, LIME AND RED PEAR JAM

1 star fruit about 175g/ 6 ounces
3 red pears total weight about 450g/ 1 pound
1 lime
½ lemon
625g/ 1 pound 6 ounces jam sugar

Chop the star fruit, core and chop the pears but do not peel them. Halve the lime. Put the fruit including the unsqueezed lime and lemon in a very large bowl. Cover and cook on Full power for 5 minutes, then stir and continue cooking for 5 minutes or until the fruit is tender but not mushy.

Using a wooden spoon press the citrus fruit against the inside of the bowl to squeeze out all the juice. Remove the squeezed peel and any stray pips.

Stir in the sugar and cook covered on Full power for 5 minutes. Stir until the sugar is dissolved. Without covering continue cooking for about 8 minutes, stirring occasionally until a little of the syrup dropped on to a chilled saucer wrinkles when pushed with a spoon. If a smoother jam is preferred it can be whizzed briefly in the blender.

Makes about 1kg/ 2¼ pounds.

This jam has a most unusual flavour which is fresher than a sweet preserve but not as sharp as a marmalade.

WEEKEND BLACKBERRY AND APPLE JAM

1 small dessert apple
225g/ 8 ounces blackberries, fresh or thawed
1 tablespoon apple juice
1 teaspoon lemon juice
225g/ 8 ounces granulated sugar
knob of butter

Peel, core and chop the apple and put in a very large bowl with the blackberries and fruit juices. Cover and cook on Full power for 3 minutes, then stir in the sugar until it is nearly dissolved. Uncover and cook for 2 minutes, then stir to make sure that the sugar has completely dissolved. Continue cooking for 5 minutes or until the jam is boiling rapidly.

Stir in the butter until melted, then cook for a further 5 minutes or until a teaspoon of the syrup dropped on to a chilled saucer wrinkles when pushed with a spoon.

Leave to cool, then spoon the jam into an attractive dish.

Makes 350g/ 12 ounces.

CHAPTER TWO

Fruit Jellies

I can never understand why even experienced preserve-makers steer clear of making jellies. In many ways they are simpler to cope with than jams and using the microwave oven they can be prepared in stages. If you wish you can cook the fruit while in the kitchen getting a meal ready, and later on when it's convenient, pour into a jelly bag or strainer over a bowl and set aside for the juice to drip through. It will not matter if it is left for a few extra hours. Next measure the juice and add a calculated weight of sugar. Finally cook at Full power until setting point is reached.

Test for setting by the wooden spoon or saucer method and skim before potting. The jelly will set more quickly in small pots and should not be shaken during cooling. Seal in the same way as jams.

In common with jam-making the set is relative to the amounts of pectin and acid in the fruit. The colour and flavour of the juice is significant, so select the fruit with this in view. Pectin and acid can be added but will alter the flavour of blander fruits.

The optimum texture is a jelly that is set without being too syrupy and only just sufficiently solid to hold its shape without liquefying. The yield is less than in jam-making because the fruit pulp is omitted. If you are not too fussy, you might care to use an unlined sieve for straining and then add some of the pulp scraped from the underside. The jelly will cloud but if you have chosen a darker, denser fruit it will not be as noticeable. Sometimes, if I have lined the sieve with a J cloth, I will gather up the edges, twist them dolly bag-fashion and give it a good squeeze. It may not be a purist's method but it does cut down the draining time. After waiting for the jelly to cool, if you find that what you thought was a good set has failed to live up to expectations, return the jelly to a bowl one size down from the one originally used and cook covered on Full power until boiling, then cook uncovered for a few minutes more. Lastly in the event of a total non-set, stir in a few tablespoons of bottled commercial pectin. The flavour may be impaired but there will be jelly to serve.

On average allow 450g/ 1 pound granulated or preserving sugar to each 600ml/ 1 pint of juice. The proportions of Jam Sugar (Sugar with pectin) are 450g/ 1 pound to 900ml/ 1½ pints of juice.

Juice from fruits that are rich in pectin can absorb approximately 25% more sugar.

APPLE JELLY

400ml/ 14 fl.oz long-life English apple juice
1 tablespoon lemon juice
450g/ 1 pound granulated sugar
6 tablespoons liquid pectin

Put the apple juice, lemon juice and sugar in a very large bowl. Cover and cook on Full power for 4 minutes, stirring occasionally. Stir until the sugar is dissolved. Without covering cook on Full power for 6 minutes or until the syrup comes to the boil. Continue cooking for a further 2 minutes.
Stir in the pectin and cook on Full power for 4 minutes. Stir and leave to cool slightly. If setting point has been reached the consistency will be loose but jelly-like. If necessary add more cooking time. Reheat for 1 minute, then pot in hot sterilized jars.

Makes about 450g/ 1 pound.

APPLE PECTIN

900g/ 2 pounds Bramley cooking apples

Rinse the apples, cut them into manageable-sized pieces and coarsely chop in the food processor. Do not peel or remove the cores. Put into a very large bowl with 300ml/ ½ pint water. Cover and cook on Full power for 10 minutes, stirring occasionally. Remove the lid, reduce the power to Medium and continue cooking for 10 minutes, or until pulped.

Line a large sieve or colander with muslin or a white J cloth and place on a rack over a very large bowl. Cover and leave to drain, pressing the pulp occasionally to extract the juice more speedily.

Put the bowl of juice in the microwave and without covering cook on Full power for 6 minutes or until reduced by half. Strain into a hot sterilized jar.

Strain into a small preserving jar and process conventionally in a water bath OR into suitably sized freezer boxes and store in the freezer after cooling. Discard the pulp.

Makes about 350ml/ 12 fl.oz.

Add to low pectin fruit when making jams or jelly. You will need about 90ml/ 3 fl.oz apple pectin for every 450g/ 1 pound of fruit.

DAMSON, MADEIRA AND ALMOND JELLY

450g/ 1 pound damsons
granulated sugar
4 tablespoons Madeira
5 tablespoons ground almonds

Rinse the damsons and put in a very large bowl with 300ml/ ½ pint water.

Cover and cook on Full power for 6 minutes or until the fruit is soft. Reduce the power to Medium and without covering cook for a further 10 minutes to bring out the flavour.

Strain through a sieve lined with a white J cloth or muslin. Measure the juice and add 100g/ 4 ounces sugar for each 150ml/ ¼ pint juice. Cover and cook for 2 minutes. Stir until the sugar is dissolved, then add the Madeira.

Without covering cook on Full power for 2 minutes or until fully boiling. Stir, then cook on Full power for 10 minutes. Mix in the ground almonds and cook for a further 5 minutes or until a few drops of the mixture placed on a chilled saucer wrinkles when pushed with a spoon.

Makes about 450g/ 1 pound.

This textured jelly is a deep wine colour and has an excellent flavour.

LOGANBERRY JELLY

450g/ 1 pound loganberries
1 tablespoon lemon juice
granulated sugar

Put the loganberries and the lemon juice in a very large bowl with 6 tablespoons water. Cover and cook on Full power for 5 minutes or until the fruit is soft.

Crush with a potato masher and rub through a sieve into another bowl. Inevitably some of the seed will come through. If cooking for a diverticulitis sufferer, first line the sieve with muslin, allow most of the juice to drain naturally, then gather the edges of the muslin and twist to expel the remainder.

Measure the volume of juice and add 100g/ 4 ounces sugar for every 150ml/ ¼ pint liquid.

Without covering cook on Full power for 2 minutes, then stir until the sugar is dissolved. Continue cooking for 2 minutes or until boiling, then cook for a further 4 minutes or until a drop of the syrup hangs from a spoon.

Makes about 450g/ 1 pound.

MOCHA AND LIME JELLY

285g/ 10 ounces granulated sugar
3 tablespoons powdered drinking chocolate
½ teaspoon vanilla flavouring
300ml/ ½ pint strong freshly made coffee
juice of 1 lime
1 tablespoon Tia Maria
8 tablespoons liquid pectin

Mix the sugar, drinking chocolate, vanilla flavouring and 6 tablespoons water in a large bowl. Cook on Full power for 2 minutes, then stir until the sugar is dissolved.

Cook until boiling (about 3 minutes), then continue cooking for a further 2 minutes.

Add the coffee, lime juice, Tia Maria and pectin and cook on Full power for 5 minutes or until a drop of the syrup hangs from the side of a spoon.

Pour into a hot sterilized jar and pot in the usual way.

Makes about 225g/ ½ pound.

PURE GRAPEFRUIT JELLY

2 large grapefruit
about 225g/ 8 ounces jam sugar
knob of butter
chopped fresh cherries (optional)

Rinse and dry the grapefruit. Finely grate the zest and set aside. Put the grapefruit in the microwave oven and cook on Full power for 1½ minutes to warm the juice, making it easier to squeeze. Cut the grapefruit in halves on a tray to catch any stray juice and squeeze the juice into a measuring jug. Add the juice from the tray.

Pour into a medium bowl and stir in 100g/ 4 ounces sugar for every 150ml/ ¼ pint. Cook on Full power for 3 minutes, stirring occasionally, add the zest, then continue cooking for 4 minutes. Stir in the butter to prevent scum forming, then continue cooking for 4 minutes or until a few drops of the syrup placed on a chilled saucer wrinkle when pushed with a spoon. Pour into a hot sterilized jam jar. Seal in the usual way. If the jelly on cooling is not thick enough cook on Full power for a few more minutes.

Store in the refrigerator and use within a week.

To add interest mix some chopped fresh cherries into the jelly before serving.

Makes about 350g/ 12 ounces.

STRAWBERRY AND REDCURRANT JELLY

450g/ 1 pound strawberries
100g/ 4 ounces redcurrants
150ml/ ¼ pint medium red wine
450g/ 1 pound granulated sugar
5 tablespoons liquid pectin

Hull the strawberries and set aside.

Put the redcurrants and wine in a very large bowl, cover and cook on Full power for 5 minutes or until the redcurrants are tender. Rub through a sieve into another bowl. Add the strawberries and sugar and cook for 2 minutes, then stir until the sugar is dissolved. Without covering cook on Full power for 4 minutes.

Stir in the pectin and cook for a further minute or until a drop of the syrup hangs from the spoon.

Makes 450g/ 1 pound.

CHAPTER THREE

Curds and Fruit Cheeses

Inarguably the microwave way is the best and most reliable method of creating foolproof curds. Gone is the need for a double saucepan or the perilous balancing of a bowl over hot water together with constant stirring. Only a basic bowl, wooden spoon and simple whisk are required.

Curds strictly speaking are not preserves, since they do not rely on sugar, pectin, or acid for their set. The vital ingredient is eggs, for it is these that are responsible for coagulation, bringing the fruit or fruit juice and sugar together to form a thick, delectable spread.

The old tried and trusty variety Lemon Curd is a national favourite probably because it is the sole variety available in most grocers. The commercial kinds vary greatly in content. The better and more expensive ones containing eggs, butter, sugar and lemon juice alone, and the worst incorporating all manner of permitted thickeners and flavourings and relying heavily on glucose syrup. The home-made lemon curd is thinner in consistency but in every other way is superior to all others.

Any conventional recipe can be adapted for microwave cookery. Measure the ingredients as stated in the recipe but follow a microwave method. One way is to put the butter into a large bowl and cook on Full power for a few seconds until melted. Stir in the sugar and most of the lemon juice and cook for a few minutes until the sugar is nearly dissolved. Beat the eggs and remaining juice, strain into the mixture, stir well, then cook on Full power, stirring frequently with a whisk to prevent curdling. A quirk of the microwave is that it cooks the mixture around the edges of the bowl more quickly than in the centre. The frequent beating mixes the hotter, more cooked part with the cooler, less cooked area, thus achieving a smooth, even, homogenous cream. Watch for a thickened bracelet of curd around the edges. This is the signal to beat vigorously. It can herald a curdle. Instant beating mixes the hot with the cool and lowers the overall temperature. It is quite magical. The entire cooking procedure can take as little as 5 minutes.

Curdling is a common occurrence in conventional curd preparation but is rare in microwave cooking. The faint-hearted may like to cook the curd on Medium power which takes a little longer and so is unlikely to go wrong.

Most curds will keep for a week in the refrigerator and for several months in the freezer although they become thinner as time goes by.

Fruit Cheeses contain no butter or eggs, consisting of fruit pulp and sugar cooked until thick. The mixture is poured into tiny dishes (a large portion is too rich) and when set firmly are unmoulded to be served as a dessert.

Fruit butters are of a soft spreading consistency. Their keeping qualities are poor but as this is primarily an 'instant' book I will not dwell on potting and sealing. However, if you do wish to store them long term, pots must be processed for hermetical sealing.

APPLE BUTTER

450g/ 1 pound cooking apples
450g/ 1 pound red-skinned dessert apples
1 cinnamon stick
½ teaspoon grated nutmeg
grated rind and juice of half a lemon
350g/ 12 ounces granulated sugar

Rinse and chop the apples. There is no need to peel or core them as they will be strained later. Put them in a very large bowl with the cinnamon stick, nutmeg, lemon rind and juice and 3 tablespoons water. Cover and cook on Full power for about 12 minutes, stirring occasionally until pulped. Press through a nylon sieve into a similar bowl (to remove the cores, cinnamon stick etc).

Cook on Full power for 2 minutes or until very hot, then stir in the sugar until beginning to dissolve. Without covering continue cooking for 8 minutes or until thick and creamy. The volume should be reduced by one half. Stir frequently as soon as the mixture starts to thicken, to prevent burning.

Spoon into hot sterilized jars, cover with waxed discs and seal in the usual way or leave until cold and serve in an attractive dish.

Makes about 450g/ 1 pound.

APRICOT AND ORANGE SPREAD

225g/ 8 ounces fresh apricots
juice and grated rind of 2 small blood oranges
50g/ 2 ounces unsalted butter
225g/ 8 ounces caster sugar
½ teaspoon orange flower water
2 large eggs

Halve and stone the apricots. Put the apricots and the orange juice and rind in a very large bowl, cover and cook on Full power for 3 minutes or until the apricots are soft.

Rub the mixture through a sieve into another bowl and stir in the butter, cut into small pieces, the sugar and the orange flower water. Stir well.

Beat the eggs with 1 tablespoon water and strain on to the mixture. Beat well with a balloon whisk.

Without covering cook on Full power for 4 minutes or until the mixture thickens. Beat after the first minute and then every 30 seconds or whenever a thickened band of the mixture appears round the edge. The spread will be just thick enough when ready to coat the back of a spoon. Remove the bowl from the microwave oven and continue beating for 3–4 minutes.

Pour into a hot sterilized jar and cover the top of the jar with cling film or a jam pot cover. If using cling film make sure that it does not come into contact with the spread.

Makes about 450g/ 1 pound.

BLUEBERRY AND CASSIS FRUIT CURD

450g / 1 pound blueberries
40g / 1½ ounces unsalted butter
225g / 8 ounces caster sugar
2 eggs
1 tablespoon cassis

Put the blueberries in a very large bowl and add 200ml / 7 fl.oz water. Cover with a vented lid or partially with cling film and cook on Full power for 5 minutes or until the fruit is soft.

Purée in the blender, then press through a nylon sieve into the bowl. Stir in the butter until melted, then mix in the sugar. Beat the eggs with a tablespoon of water and strain on to the mixture.

Cook uncovered on Full power for 3 minutes, beating with a whisk every 30 seconds. Test with a spoon handle which should momentarily leave a trail when drawn through the mixture.

If necessary continue cooking on Low power, beating frequently. A curdle is less likely to occur when cooked on Low. Stir in the cassis.

Makes about 450g / 1 pound.

DAMSON AND GRAPE CHEESE

450g / 1 pound damsons
100g / 4 ounces juicy green grapes
granulated sugar

Put the damsons and the grapes in a very large bowl with 4 tablespoons water. Cover and cook on Full power for 10 minutes or until the fruit is soft. Stir occasionally. The grapes may explode but will come to no harm if the lid is in place. Crush down with a potato masher to help release the juice, then rub through a sieve into another bowl, scraping in all the pulp from the underside of the sieve.

Weigh the pulp and add an equal weight of sugar. Replace the mixture in the very large bowl and cook on Full power for 3 minutes. Stir until the sugar is dissolved. Reduce the power to Medium and without covering cook for 15 minutes or until the mixture thickens. Watch the mixture closely during the second half of the cooking time as burning can occur if the mixture dries out too much. Spoon into tiny individual moulds or ramekins. Seal with waxed discs and jam pot covers unless the dessert is to be served within a day.

To serve, loosen with a hot, wet, round-bladed knife, turn out on to small plates and surround with cream. Ice cream or Pompadour wafers would complement this dessert.

Makes enough for 6 – 10 servings.

GOOSEBERRY AND KIWI CURD

225g/8 ounces gooseberries
2 tablespoons sweet white wine
3 large eggs
100g/ 4 ounces granulated sugar
50g/ 2 ounces unsalted butter
2 small kiwi fruit

Top and tail and halve the gooseberries and put them in a large bowl with 2 tablespoons water. Cover and cook on Full power for 5 minutes or until soft. Stir occasionally to ensure even cooking.

Pour the gooseberries into the blender and process until smooth. Add the wine, pulse once or twice, then add the eggs and pulse briefly until well blended. Place a sieve over the bowl and pour in the mixture, pressing with a wooden spoon. Stir in the sugar and add the butter cut into small pieces. Without covering cook on Full power for 4 minutes, stirring briskly every 30 seconds. Continue cooking, beating every 15 seconds until the curd thickens. A wooden spoon moved paddle fashion through the mixture should meet with some resistance.

Peel, slice and mash the kiwi fruit and press through a small strainer into the thickened curd. Cook on Medium power for 30 seconds. Beat with a whisk until cool.

When cold, the curd will thicken further. Since the kiwi fruit is barely cooked it is advisable to serve within 24 hours. Refrigerate during this time.

Makes about 450g/ 1 pound.

NECTARINE CHEESE

4 nectarines, total weight 450g/ 1 pound
¼ teaspoon ground mixed spice
¼ teaspoon ground cloves
granulated sugar

Peel the nectarines. Slice the flesh into a large bowl and add 120ml/ 4 fl.oz water. Discard the stones.
Cover and cook on Full power until tender (about 5 minutes).
Purée in the blender or press through a nylon sieve. Measure the purée, then return to the bowl, adding 75g/ 3 oz of sugar for every 120ml/ 4 fl. oz purée.
Stir in mixed spice and cloves. Cook on Full power for 2 minutes, then stir until the sugar is dissolved. Uncover and continue cooking, stirring frequently, for about 10 minutes or until the mixture is thick and a spoon handle drawn through the mixture leaves a furrow.

Makes 285g/ 10 ounces.

RASPBERRY CURD

350g / 12 ounces raspberries
100g / 4 ounces granulated sugar
50g / 2 ounces unsalted butter
2 eggs plus 2 egg yolks

Put the raspberries in a large bowl, cover and cook on Full power for 3 minutes or until the juices begin to flow. Remove the lid and continue cooking for 5 minutes or until the liquid is reduced by one-third. The mixture can be strained at this stage if a seedless curd is preferred.

Stir in the sugar until dissolved. Add the butter in small pieces and stir until melted. Beat the eggs and yolks together and add two tablespoons of the raspberry syrup. Strain into the mixture and stir thoroughly.

Reduce the setting to Medium power and without covering cook for 4 minutes or until the curd thickens, beating with a whisk every 30 seconds to avoid curdling. The mixture must be beaten each time a thickened ring of the curd appears around the edges of the bowl. Continue whisking until the curd is cool.

Seal and pot if wished or spoon into an attractive dish. Keeps if covered and refrigerated for one week.

Makes about 450g / 1 pound.

Frozen raspberries may be substituted and should be cooked from their frozen state to prevent loss of valuable juices. Allow a longer initial cooking time as frozen fruit takes longer than fresh.

REDUCED SUGAR LIME CURD

2 large eggs
grated rind and juice of 4 limes
75g/ 3 ounces granulated sugar
50g/ 2 ounces polyunsaturated margarine
green food colouring (optional)

Beat the eggs and lime juice together and strain into a large bowl. Add the grated lime rind, sugar and margarine. Mix well.

Cook on Full power for 1 minute, then continue cooking for a further 2 minutes, whisking frequently and immediately each time a thickened band of the curd appears around the edges.

Continue cooking if necessary until a fork drawn through the mixture leaves a trail. Add a drop of food colouring if wished.

Remove from the microwave and continue beating for 3 minutes, then pour into an attractive jar or dish.

Cover and refrigerate and consume within 24 hours. The curd thickens as it cools.

Makes about 350g/ 12 ounces.

SPARKLING LEMON CURD

3 lemons
2 large eggs
100g/ 4 ounces caster sugar
50g/ 2 ounces unsalted butter

Squeeze the juice from 2 of the lemons. Grate the rind from the other, then remove the pith, membranes and pips. Chop and set aside the flesh.

Beat the eggs and lemon juice together and strain into a medium sized bowl. Stir in the sugar and add the butter, cut into cubes. Cook on Full power for about 4 minutes or until the curd thickens when a spoon handle drawn through the mixture leaves a trail, beating with a whisk every 30 seconds. The first sign of thickening is a bracelet of the curd which appears around the edges of the mixture. It is imperative to beat every time this becomes visible to prevent curdling and mix the cool and hot parts together.

Stir in the reserved chopped lemon and the grated rind and cook for a further minute, stirring every 20 seconds.

Makes about 350g/ 12 ounces.

CHAPTER FOUR

Whole Preserved Fruit and Spiced Fruit

Conventional fruit bottling is fraught with hazards. Jars must be scrupulously examined with any even slightly damaged discarded. They must be absolutely clean and treated with the utmost care. Instructions must be followed to the letter, do not tighten screw bands before processing, but be sure to do this immediately after processing. Leave the bands in position until the bottles are completely cold. Observe the processing temperature and timing exactly and always put a rack in the water-bath.

Given all these do's and don'ts it is hardly surprising that the microwave cannot be used for bottling. But happily the microwave oven can do much of the tedious preparation. Used in conjunction with the freezer, similar results to bottling can be obtained without all the bottling rigmarole. Make the syrups in the microwave, heat the fruit in the microwave and providing the jars are completely airtight and filled to the brim, refrigerator storage in the short term is acceptable.

Fruit preserved in a high ratio sugar syrup or steeped in a goodly quantity of alcohol, be it vodka, brandy or similar high proof liquors, keep well as these drinks are preservatives in themselves. Fruit bottled in water alone or in a light syrup must be subsequently processed conventionally.

Fruits such as peaches should be skinned before cooking but plums, greengages and the like require only a good rinse. Sliced fruit creates its own juice which oozes into the syrup or alcohol, while at the same time absorbing flavour from the liquid it is infused in.

Spiced fruit, as the description implies, is prepared mostly with whole spices such as cinnamon sticks and cloves. Whole spices can easily be retrieved whereas ground spices cannot. The latter are inclined to cloud the preserving liquid although I have been mostly successful in straining them away.

Spiced fruit is adaptable and can be served either as a dessert or with cold meats and fish.

CARDAMOM SPICED ORANGES

3 medium oranges
6 green cardamom pods
1 fresh lovage leaf
200ml/ 7 fl.oz cider vinegar
6 cloves
175g/ 6 ounces granulated sugar

Wash and thinly slice the oranges but not so thinly that they are floppy. Bruise the cardamom pods and snip the lovage leaf with scissors. Set aside.

Put the orange slices into a large bowl with 225ml/ 8 fl.oz hot water. Cover and cook on Full power for 10 minutes or until the rinds are tender. Drain the oranges and set aside. Throw away the water.

Put the reserved cardamoms, the lovage and the sugar in the bowl and without covering cook on Full power for 2 minutes. Stir until the sugar is dissolved, then continue cooking for 3 minutes or until boiling.

Reduce the power to Medium and without covering cook for 15 minutes or until the rinds are translucent.

Remove the orange slices with a slotted spoon and layer in a hot sterilized jar. Leave the syrup in the bowl, raise the power to Full and cook for 3 minutes or until the syrup thickens to the density of the heavy syrup in canned fruit. Pour over the orange slices and press the fruit down to expel any air bubbles. The syrup should cover the fruit. Seal and pot in the usual way.

Makes about 450g/ 1 pound.

FIGS IN BRANDY

16 well shaped whole dried figs
100g / 4 ounces granulated sugar
1 teaspoon cumin seeds
300ml / ½ pint brandy

Rinse and dry the figs but do not remove the stalks. Put into a very large bowl with the sugar and cumin seeds. Cover and cook on Full power for 2 minutes. Reduce the power to Medium and continue cooking for 10 minutes. Leave to stand for 2 hours.

Strain the syrup into another bowl, pack the figs into hot sterilized jars and half fill with brandy.

Put the bowl of syrup in the microwave and without covering cook on Full power for 7 minutes or until reduced by half.

Pour through a funnel on to the figs, filling the jars to within 1cm / ½ inch of the rim. Seal tightly with lids. Reverse the jars once or twice to mix the brandy and syrup completely. Store in a cool, dry, dark place for 3 weeks before using.

Makes 2 × 350g / 12 ounce jars.

HONEYED GREENGAGES

4 tablespoons clear honey
175g/ 6 ounces granulated sugar
675g/ 1½ pounds greengages

Put the honey, sugar and 175ml/ 6 fl.oz water in a large bowl. Cook on Full power for 3 minutes, then stir until the sugar is dissolved. Continue cooking until boiling (about 3 minutes) then for an additional 2 minutes.

Wash and pierce the greengages and put into the syrup. Reduce the power to Defrost and cook for 10 minutes or until the fruit is thoroughly hot but still holds its shape. Transfer the greengages to a hot sterilized preserving jar. Reheat the syrup in the microwave on Full power until boiling once more (about 2 minutes) and immediately pour over the fruit through a funnel leaving a 1cm/ ½ inch headspace. Follow instructions for conventional bottling, allowing 15 minutes in the water bath.

Makes about 675g/ 1½ pounds.

PINEAPPLE IN CURAÇAO

1 small pineapple
375g/ 12 ounces granulated sugar
300ml/½ pint Curaçao
vodka
extra sugar

Peel, pit and core the pineapple, then put whole into a large bowl. Add 200ml/ 7 fl.oz water, cover and cook on Full power for 5 minutes or until the fruit is thoroughly hot. Turn the pineapple over, cover and continue cooking for 2 minutes. Carefully remove the pineapple and place in a plastic colander set over a bowl to catch the drips.

Stir the sugar into the liquid remaining in the bowl and without covering cook on Full power for 2 minutes. Stir until dissolved, then cook until boiling (about 2 minutes). Continue cooking for 3 minutes or until the syrup is about as thick as syrup from canned fruit.

Add the collected pineapple juice and the Curaçao. Stand the pineapple in an earthenware pot and pour the syrup over it. If the syrup does not cover the pineapple it will not preserve safely.

Top up with vodka which is flavourless and cover with a well fitting pottery lid. Next day turn the pineapple over and add 2-3 tablespoons sugar.

Consume after one week. Check each day, adding extra sugar and vodka if needed.

Makes enough for 6 servings.

PITTED CHERRIES IN HONEY SYRUP

450g/ 1 pound red cherries
450g/ 1 pound white cherries
175g/ 6 ounces granulated sugar
50g/ 2 ounces clear honey

Rinse and dry the cherries and remove the stalks and stones. It is best to use a cherry stoner so that the fruit remains whole.

Pack the cherries in a snugly fitting freezer box and put in the freezer to chill.

Mix the sugar with 300ml/ ½ pint water, cover and cook on Full power for 2 minutes. Stir in the honey and without covering cook for 2 minutes or until boiling. Continue cooking for 2 minutes, then slowly stir in 300ml/ ½ pint of water.

When the syrup is cool, pour into the cherries, making sure that they are totally covered. To make sure, crumple a piece of foil and press it down on top. Put on the lid and store in the freezer for up to 12 months.

To thaw, remove the lid and put the reversed box in a bowl sufficiently large to accommodate the fruit when defrosted. Cook on Full power for 2 minutes, press lightly on the freezer box to eject the frozen fruit. Reduce the power to Very Low (level 1) and cook for 15 minutes or until nearly thawed. To hasten the process, carefully break up the block with a fork to allow the thawed syrup to flow.

Makes enough for 6–8 servings.

PRESERVED KUMQUATS

350g/ 12 ounces kumquats
¼ teaspoon almond essence
350g/ 12 ounces granulated sugar
2 tablespoons Grand Marnier

Rinse and dry the kumquats, remove the tiny hard stalks and spear with the tip of a sharp knife to prevent the fruit from bursting. Put the kumquats in a large bowl with 5 tablespoons water and the almond essence. Cover and cook on Full power for 4 minutes to soften the skins of the fruit. Overcooking at this stage will cause them to collapse.

Remove the fruit with a slotted spoon and stir the sugar into the juices remaining in the bowl. Add 200ml/ 7 fl.oz water. Cook on Full power for 2 minutes, stir, then continue cooking for 5 minutes or until a thin syrup is formed. Return the fruit to the bowl.

Cover and cook on Full power for 9 minutes or until the syrup is of similar density to bottled syrup and a pale orange colour. Take care not to overcook or the syrup will caramelise and may burn. Leave for a few moments, then stir in the Grand Marnier. Spoon the fruit into hot sterilized jars and fill to the rim with syrup. Place the jars one at a time in the microwave and cook for 15 seconds or until the syrup almost boils over. Remove the jars with oven or rubber gloves, then wipe and seal immediately.

Enough for 2 × 225g/ ½ pound jars.

The kumquats will keep either in the refrigerator or freezer for two to three weeks if stored in a suitable freezer box. During storage the syrup will thicken further.

SWEET AND SOUR GINGER PEACHES

75g/ 3 ounces crystallized ginger
1 cinnamon stick
2 teaspoons salt
½ teaspoon citric acid crystals
6 firm small freestone peaches
350g/ 12 ounces preserving sugar
150ml/ ¼ pint red wine vinegar

Slice the ginger and break the cinnamon stick into 4 pieces and set aside. Dissolve the salt and citric acid crystals in about 600ml/ 1 pint cold water.

Immerse the peaches in a bowl of boiling water for 2 minutes to loosen the skins. Remove with a slotted spoon, then rub off the skins. Immediately plunge the peaches in the salty acidulated water and turn them over. Cover tightly.

Put the sugar and vinegar in a very large bowl, cover and cook on Full power for 3 minutes. Stir until the sugar is dissolved. Without covering cook until boiling (about 2 minutes), then continue cooking for a further 2 minutes.

Add the peaches to the bowl of syrup and coat them thoroughly. Cook on Full power for 1 minute or until the syrup comes back to the boil. Add the broken cinnamon stick.

Put a plate on top of the fruit and stand a dish of water on top to weight it down – a pint of water weighs a pound. Cover and leave for 24 hours. Remove the weighted dish and plate, then cover the bowl and cook on Full power for 3 minutes or until boiling. Leave for a minute or two to allow the fruit to continue cooking in the residual heat, then lift out the peaches with a slotted spoon. Without covering cook the syrup on Full power for 4 minutes or until the consistency of heavy syrup. Replace the peaches and cook until the syrup comes back to the boil. Transfer the fruit and cinnamon to a hot sterilized jar, stir in the ginger and fill to the brim with syrup. Press down the

61

fruit with a spoon, then pot in the usual way.

After cooling, store in the refrigerator. The syrup must cover the fruit so it is a good idea to turn the jar over (assuming that it is well sealed) every day. Use after 1 week.

Makes enough for 6 servings.

WHISKEY TIPPLE APRICOTS

15–18 firm but ripe apricots
350g/ 12 ounces granulated sugar
300ml/ ½ pint Irish whiskey

Rinse and dry the apricots. Put the sugar in a very large bowl and add 250ml/ 8 fl.oz boiling water. Cover and cook on Full power for 2 minutes or until boiling. Without covering cook on Full power for 3 minutes, then add the apricots. Continue cooking for 2 minutes or until the apricots are hot throughout but not softly cooked.

Pack the fruit into 2 or 3 jars and divide the whiskey between them. Cook the syrup on Full power for 10 minutes or until the consistency of heavy syrup.

Pour into the jars until they are full to the brim. Seal and pot in the usual way.

When cool, store in the refrigerator for two weeks. Once opened consume within a day or two.

Makes enough for 5–6 servings.

CHAPTER FIVE

Candied and Crystallized Fruit

Candied fruit can either be eaten as a sweetmeat or chopped and added to puddings or cake mixtures. A wide strip of candied lemon peel is traditionally placed on Madeira cake half-way through cooking and the much favoured Italian cassata ice cream is speckled with fragments of candied mixed peel. The outer layer of peel from citrus fruit is the most widely used.

Although no special recipe has been included, angelica stalks are candied and used to flavour and decorate cakes. Angelica is an ancient herb and was believed to be an antidote to witches' spells and a *remedye* for the plague.

The process for making candied fruit is similar whichever recipe is used. After softening, the peel is cooked in syrup and left to steep for several hours. It is then removed from the syrup which is further boiled to reduce and thicken it. This process is repeated a few times after which the peel is arranged on a rack to dry. The microwave is used at each stage and is infinitely less messy. The bowl can be tucked away in an unobtrusive place during the waiting times.

Crystallized or sugared fruit or nuts are prepared in a similar way, the sugared effect being achieved either by dipping whole fruit or unskinned segments into thick syrup cooked to high temperature or by rolling the pieces in granulated sugar after cooking. When the cooled nuts are dipped in hot syrup they acquire a frosted appearance.

Candying and crystallising is admittedly fiddly and will not appeal to anyone lacking patience and expecting instant results, but nevertheless success imparts a great deal of satisfaction and makes up for all the tedium.

CANDIED GRAPES

175g/ 6 ounces large grapes, black or green
100g/ 4 ounces granulated sugar
1 teaspoon powdered glucose

Wash and dry the grapes thoroughly but do not remove their stalks. Divide into pairs joined together by the stalks. This makes them easier to dip and achieve the speed necessary for success. Line a baking tray with non-stick parchment and place on a heat-proof surface.

Put the sugar and glucose in a large jug or medium bowl and stir in 5 tablespoons of water. Cook on Full power for 1 minute, stir, then continue cooking for 4–6 minutes or until a sugar thermometer registers 155°C/310°F when 'crack' stage is reached and a little of the syrup poured into cold water separates into brittle strands. DO NOT STIR DURING THIS STAGE OF COOKING. Bear in mind that in microwave cooking the temperature of syrups rises rapidly even after removal from the microwave oven. When approaching this temperature the syrup thickens visibly and the colour darkens slightly.

Using a fork, quickly dip the grapes into the syrup one pair at a time, making sure that they are completely coated.

Arrange well separated on the prepared tray and leave for 5 minutes or until completely set.

The candied fruit must be kept in a warm dry atmosphere. If there is any humidity the brittle coating will start to melt.

Makes about 12 pairs.

CANDIED PEEL

3 oranges, washed and dried
2 lemons, washed and dried
550g/ 1¼ pounds granulated sugar
3 tablespoons golden syrup
¼ teaspoon ground ginger

Halve the fruit and squeeze the juice into a measuring jug. Scoop out the membrane and pips, cut the peel into strips and remove most of the pith. Slice the peel into strips. Put into a medium bowl, add cold water to cover and cook on Full power until boiling (about 2 minutes). Continue cooking for a further 2 minutes. Drain and replace the strips in the bowl, covering with water as before but this time cook for 3 minutes after boiling point is reached and do not drain until required.

Line a baking sheet with non-stick parchment and cover with 100g/ 4 ounces of the sugar. Combine the remainder with the syrup and ginger in a very large bowl, add the juice and make up to 300ml/ ½ pint with boiling water. Stir until the sugar is dissolved. Without covering cook on Full power for 10 minutes. Reduce the power to Medium, drain and stir in the peel, then cook for 10 minutes or until the syrup is thick and mostly absorbed by the peel. Check frequently during cooking to make sure the mixture does not burn, which can happen quickly as it begins to thicken. Using tongs transfer the strips individually, spreading them out in a single layer on the prepared tray. Toss to coat well. Leave for several hours, then layer between waxed paper in an airtight container.

Consume within one week.

Makes about 225g/ 8 ounces.

MARRONS GLACÉS

675g/ 1½ pounds large chestnuts
350g/ 12 ounces granulated sugar
350g/ 12 ounces powdered glucose
1 teaspoon vanilla flavouring

Slit the chestnuts through the curved side and put in a very large bowl. Add 300ml/ ½ pint boiling water. Cover and cook on Full power for 2 minutes or until the water comes back to the boil. Stir so that the chestnuts at the bottom come to the top, then continue cooking for 3 minutes or until the shells open.

Leave to stand for 10 minutes to ensure that the chestnuts are tender, then remove the peel and the brown skin.

Mix the sugar, glucose, vanilla flavouring and 300ml/ ½ pint water in a very large bowl, cover and cook on Full power for 3 minutes. Stir until the sugar and glucose are dissolved. Without covering cook on Full power for 5 minutes or until the mixture comes to the boil. Stir and continue cooking for 2 minutes to slightly thicken the syrup, then add the chestnuts. Cover and set aside in a warm place for 24 hours.

After this period and without covering cook on Full power for 5 minutes or until boiling, then continue cooking for 2 minutes.

Leave for 24 hours, then repeat the last process but reduce the cooking times as boiling point will be reached more quickly.

Using a slotted spoon remove the chestnuts from the syrup and place on a wire rack over a tray to catch the drips. Add the drips to any remaining syrup and cook on Full power until boiling rapidly. Remove from the microwave. Dip each chestnut in boiling water and then into the thickened syrup. Spread the chestnuts out on a non-stick baking tray and leave in a dry atmosphere until cold. Wrap individually in waxed paper or foil.

Makes 15 to 25 depending on the size of the chestnuts.

SUGARED WALNUTS

225g/ 8 ounces walnut halves
300g/ 11 ounces granulated sugar

Put the walnuts in a medium bowl, cover with cold water and cook on Full power for 5 minutes or until boiling. Drain, rinse and pat dry in a clean tea cloth.

In a large bowl mix 225g/ 8 ounces of the sugar with 150ml/ ¼ pint water. Without covering cook on Full power for 3 minutes. Stir and continue cooking for 2 minutes or until syrupy and only just coloured.

Remove the bowl from the microwave, stir in the nuts and when well coated with syrup, remove them with a slotted spoon and place in a colander set over a tray to catch the drips.

Replace the bowl of syrup in the microwave and cook on Full power for 2 minutes to reheat. Immerse the nuts and remove and drain as before.

Cook the syrup on Full power for 2 minutes, then add the remaining sugar. Stir well and continue cooking for 5 minutes. Replace the nuts and stir to coat them thoroughly. A crisp sugary crust may form. Spread the sugared walnuts out on a wire rack placed over a baking tray and leave in a warm spot to dry. A low oven for half an hour should do the trick.

Store in a tightly lidded box in a cool dry place. A tiny parcel of white kitchen paper packed with uncooked rice, tucked in a corner of the box will help to keep the nuts crisp.

Makes about 225g/ 8 ounces.

CHAPTER SIX

Syrups for Bottling and Preserves

Bottling in the true sense requires that the fruit and syrup having been packed into preserving jars, are covered with their lids and sealed loosely with either screw tops or clip tops. The jars are then put in a water bath either on the hob or on folded newspaper in a conventional oven. Here they are brought slowly up to a certain temperature at which they are held for a specified time. During this period all the air which would be the cause of deterioration is driven out. Immediately after removal the tops are tightened to form a perfect seal after the jars have cooled down.

Bottling in the microwave oven is not recommended. Even though I believe plastic tops are available, any tightly lidded container albeit a non-metallic one, is dangerous to use particularly when there is a pronounced risk of boiling over. At boiling point or very soon after, the lid will shoot off and a glass jar would explode and could indeed severely damage the microwave oven. My second reason for forbidding bottling in the microwave is that the temperature of the contents cannot be measured with a lid in place. Due to the distribution of the microwaves, were more than one jar to be heated simultaneously in the microwave, the likelihood of reaching equivalent temperatures is even less. Microwave bottling even if it were bacterially safe, would be impractical as so few jars could be fitted into the microwave oven's small cavity.

Bottling was a useful method of preservation in times past when fruit was all home-grown and specific varieties only available in season. When there was a glut of fruit there was no other means of storage without deterioration. Bottling was *de rigueur* before the arrival of the freezer. Nowadays most consumers prefer to use this indispensable appliance to preserve fruit without the need for lengthy processing. Bottles take up a lot of space and few houses have a walk-in larder. To maximise space use square or rectangular shaped freezer cartons each containing the portions required.

The microwave can be employed to distinct advantage by using it to prepare the syrups for bottling and for freezing, for ice cream and cordials. The microwave method is the most convenient and cleanest

70

way to make syrups of all descriptions. The sugar dissolves more easily and changes in colour and density are simpler to monitor as they are prepared in see-through Pyrex or similar glass. Syrups, if properly covered, store well in the refrigerator.

BLACKTHORN SYRUP

450g/ 1 pound sloes
granulated sugar

Put the sloes in a very large bowl and just cover with water. Cover with a lid and cook on Full power for 2 minutes or until boiling. Stir and without covering continue cooking for 3 minutes.
Cover and leave in a cool place for 12 or more hours.
Remove the sloes and set aside. Cover the bowl of juice and cook on Full power for 2 minutes or until boiling. Replace the sloes and continue cooking for two minutes or until the syrup returns to the boil.
Leave covered until cold. Discard the sloes.
Measure the juice and stir in 225g/ 8 ounces sugar for each 600ml/ 1 pint of juice. Cook on Full power for 2 minutes or until boiling. Stir and boil for a further minute. Immediately pour through a funnel into hot sterilized bottles and seal with corks.

Makes about 600ml/ 1 pint.

Sloes are tiny wild plums and are not edible raw. Gather them while blue and wear plastic gloves to avoid staining your hands.

LEMON CORDIAL

grated rind and juice of 4 large lemons
225g/ 8 ounces granulated sugar

Put the grated lemon rind in a large jug with 12 tablespoons water. Cover and cook on full power for 3 minutes. Reduce the power to Medium and without covering cook for a further 7 minutes.
Strain into a large bowl and stir in the sugar until beginning to dissolve. Add the lemon juice.
Without covering cook on Full power for 4 minutes or until boiling rapidly. Stir, then continue cooking for a further 2 minutes or until syrupy.
Pour into a hot sterilized bottle or jar. Leave to cool, then put on the lid and store in the refrigerator.

Serve diluted with iced water in the proportion of 1:5.

Makes 400ml/ 14 fl.oz.

LEMON SORBET

600ml/ 1 pint sorbet syrup (page 75)
grated rind and juice of 4 lemons
juice of 2 oranges
2 teaspoons powdered gelatine (or vegetarian equivalent)
1 egg white (or reconstituted pasteurised dried egg white powder)

Put the syrup in a large bowl, add the grated lemon rind, cover and set aside to steep for two hours. Add the lemon and orange juices.

In a small bowl or jug mix the gelatine with 4 tablespoons water. Heat on Full power to steaming point about 45 seconds. Stir until completely dissolved, then leave to cool down. If left for too long the gelatine will set and it is essential that it remains liquid.

As soon as it is ready, stir into the lemon syrup. Mix thoroughly and pour into a freezer box. Cover with the lid and deep freeze until icy yet slushy (about 2 hours). Return the mixture to the bowl and beat preferably with an electric whisk at minimum speed. The mixture will change colour and increase in volume.

Turn the mixture into the freezer box, then freeze again. Expect this stage to take about 1 hour. Whisk once more, gradually increasing the speed. Using clean beaters and a grease-free bowl whisk the egg white to soft peaks, then fold into the sorbet. Freeze until required, then transfer to the refrigerator for 15 minutes (the time depends on the size of the portions being frozen) before serving.

Makes about 900ml/ 1½ pints.

RASPBERRY AND ORANGE SYRUP

450g/ 1 pound raspberries
juice of 2 oranges
175g/ 6 ounces granulated sugar
½ teaspoon rose water (optional)

Put the raspberries in a large bowl, cover and cook on Full power for 2 minutes or until the juices flow freely. Press through a sieve into a similar sized bowl. Add the orange juice and sugar and stir well. Cook on Full power for 3 minutes, then stir until the sugar is dissolved. Without covering continue cooking for 2 minutes or until boiling. Stir and cook for a further minute or until a light syrupy consistency.
Immediately pour through a funnel into a hot sterilized bottle. Cork at once.

Makes about 450ml/¾ pint.

The addition of a half teaspoon of rosewater to the syrup will impart a delicately perfumed aroma.

SORBET SYRUP

300g/ 11 ounces granulated sugar
600ml/ 1 pint boiling water

Put the sugar in a large bowl, add the water whilst boiling and stir thoroughly until dissolved. Without covering cook on Full power until the syrup is reduced to 600ml/ 1 pint. It is a good idea first to mark the 600ml/ 1 pint level on the outside of the bowl.
Use when cool.
If you wish to bottle the syrup follow the directions for conventional bottling.

Makes 600ml/ 1 pint.

STOCK SYRUP

225g/ 8 ounces granulated sugar

Put the sugar in a medium bowl and stir in 150ml/ ¼ pint water. Cover and cook on Full power for 1 minute, then stir until the sugar is dissolved.
Without covering cook on Full power for 1 minute or until boiling rapidly, then continue cooking for a further 2 minutes.
Leave to cool, then pour into a bottle or screw-top jar.

Makes about 300ml/ ½ pint.

Stored in the refrigerator the syrup will keep for several weeks.
Use as required to sweeten thawed, freshly cooked fruit or fruit salad.
Add liqueur if wished.

STRAWBERRY COINTREAU SORBET

600ml/ 1 pint sorbet syrup
4 tablespoons lemon juice
4 tablespoons orange juice
900g/ 2 pounds ripe strawberries
1 tablespoon Cointreau

Pour the syrup into a large bowl and add the lemon and orange juice. Rinse, drain and hull the strawberries and purée in the blender. Press through a nylon sieve into the syrup. Mix in the Cointreau.

Pour into a freezer box, cover and deep freeze until icy yet slushy (about 2 hours). Purée in the blender in two or three batches, then freeze in the portions required.

Transfer to the refrigerator for 15 minutes or leave at room temperature for 10 minutes, then serve using an ice-cream scoop that has been dipped in cold water.

Makes about 1 litre/ 1¾ pints.

There are no stabilisers such as gelatine or egg white in this recipe, resulting in a coarser texture. Serve two scoops per person and garnish with two or three whole fresh strawberries and if possible a strawberry leaf.

SYRUPS FOR BOTTLING

The ratio of sugar to water must be correct to achieve the density of syrups required for bottling. This chart gives an indication of the quantity of syrup needed to cover 900g/ 2 pounds of stoned fruit. Whole fruit takes up more space and so needs less syrup.

Syrup	Boiling Water	Sugar
Light	600ml/ 1 pint	225g/ 8 ounces
Medium	500ml/ 18 fl.oz	200g/ 7 ounces
Medium Heavy	500ml/ 18 fl.oz	300g/ 10 ounces
Heavy	450ml/ ¾ pint	350g/ 12 ounces

The use of boiling water is recommended as it takes much longer to boil larger amounts of water in the microwave than in the kettle. There is unavoidably a short lapse of time between pouring the water into the bowl and starting cooking in the microwave. During this period the water will drop below boiling point.

Put the sugar into the bowl in advance to avoid too much drop in temperature. Pour in the boiling water, then cover and cook on Full power for 2 minutes. Stir until the sugar is dissolved.
Without covering cook on Full power for 4 – 8 minutes or until fast boiling, then continue cooking for about 2 minutes. To make a cold syrup use half the amount of boiling water, which cuts down the cooking time, and add the balance in cold water after the syrup has cooled slightly.

CHAPTER SEVEN

Savoury Jellies

Complement sliced cold collations of sliced meats and poultry, game and oily fish and vegetarian items like cutlets, sliced tomatoes and hard-boiled eggs with a drift of sparkling fresh savoury jelly spooned on the side of the plate or arranged as a garnish on individual items.

Prepared in a similar way to fruit jellies, the savoury varieties comprise more piquant ingredients and the majority incorporate herbs. Savoury jellies are less sweet and the 'gel' is looser. In the event of the completed jelly being too sloppy it can be further thickened with gelatine or in the case of vegetarian food, agar-agar. Melt the jelly in the microwave oven set on Medium power, then measure the volume and return it to the bowl. Make up the gelatine or agar-agar solution with a little water or liquefied jelly in about half the proportion stated on the packet. Add to the bowl and bring back to the boil on Full power. The jelly will thicken on cooling. It is likely that by this time all the herbs have been subject to some cooking. So chop some extra fresh herbs and stir into the jelly when almost set.

Neither the flavour and certainly not the texture of dried herbs can compare with fresh, bright, crisp aromatic herbs that are grown in window boxes or cultivated in the garden. Practically every large supermarket has a display of rosemary, basil, thyme, parsley and sage. They are not too expensive and almost become a bargain if you intend to nurture them, otherwise remove the number of leaves desired and freeze the remainder, preferably in water as ice cubes. Stored this way the herbs may well become limp but they do retain much of their colour and the flavour is unimpaired. Also a herbed ice cube stirred into the cool jelly will speed the setting time.

Growing and tending herbs

Keen experienced gardeners are fully conversant with the art of herb growing but I write this paragraph for the totally ignorant amateur like myself who, although having always taken an enthusiastic interest in using culinary herbs, had until recently learnt nothing about growing and looking after them.

My interest was awakened when I first spotted the supermarket cartons of fresh herbs. They were already growing in their little plastic tubs of compost and I only needed to situate them in the right position and water as and when instructed. Apparently basil, chervil, chives, parsley and thyme are good choices for window boxes as they are non-invasive and don't go spreading their roots all over the place. Mint, which seems to flourish anywhere, has roots which creep sideways just under the soil to reappear and multiply in an alarming fashion. The ready to plant supermarket kind can be removed from the containers and then sunk into a suitably sized hole in a pot of herb compost. Press the compost around the plant and after the initial generous watering, add water sparingly. Treat indoor herbs in the same manner as house-plants. Give them plenty of ventilation, keep them away from draughts, not too wet and not too dry. It is unlikely that you will wish to grow herbs in large quantities and only limited amounts are used in cooking. To keep them happy, pop a little green fertiliser pill into each pot and water over it each time moisture is needed. When the roots start protruding through the bottom hole in the pot, it is time to transfer the plant to a larger pot.

Some garden soils are more suitable for herb growing than others and if you are fortunate to have an agreeable patch in a reasonably sunny yet sheltered spot, you can become more adventurous. Grow from seed if you have enough faith or go to a well-stocked garden centre or specialist herb nursery and plant some of the less common varieties. Bergamot, used in one of the recipes, grows contentedly in a partly shaded position and lovage positively thrives in these conditions – but be warned, lovage can sprout rapidly, soon becoming a very large bush indeed. Herb growing is both a rewarding and obsessive hobby and certainly increases one's savoury jelly repertoire.

CELERY LEAF JELLY

2 handfuls celery leaves
175ml/ 6 fl.oz cider
450g/ 1 pound granulated sugar
5 tablespoons liquid pectin

Finely chop the celery leaves and put into a bowl with 4 tablespoons water. Cook on Full power for 2 minutes or until boiling. Cover and set aside for 30 minutes to infuse.

Meanwhile put the cider and sugar in a very large bowl and stir well. Cover and cook on Full power for 2 minutes, then stir until the sugar is dissolved.

Strain in the herb infusion, and without covering cook on Full power for 4 minutes. Stir in the pectin and continue cooking for 2 minutes or until a little of the liquid placed on a chilled saucer wrinkles when pushed with a spoon.

Makes about 550g/ 1¼ pounds.

Celery leaf has a slightly sharper flavour than the leaves on celery bunches. Lovage, although different in flavour, could be substituted. It is similar in appearance.

CLEAR BERGAMOT JELLY

2 handfuls bergamot leaves
450g/ 1 pound cooking apples
200ml/ 7 fl.oz white malt vinegar
preserving sugar

Set aside and finely chop one quarter of the bergamot leaves. Put the remainder in a large bowl with 200ml/ 7 fl.oz water. Rinse and coarsely chop the apples (including the peel and cores) and stir into the water. Cover and cook on Full power for 7 minutes or until pulped. Stirring once or twice during cooking speeds the process. Stir in the vinegar and cook for a further 5 minutes. Cover and leave until cold. Line a large nylon sieve with a double layer of clean muslin and place over another bowl. Pour the mixture into the sieve, cover and leave to drain. Allow at least 3 hours and resist the temptation to press the pulp through.

Measure the juice and add 225g/ 8 ounces sugar to every 300ml/ ½ pint liquid. Without covering cook on Full power for 5 minutes, then stir until the sugar is dissolved. Continue cooking for 15 minutes or until setting point is reached.

Skim away any white scum, leave to cool slightly, then stir in the reserved bergamot leaves.

Pour through a funnel into hot sterilized jars. Seal as usual.

Enough to fill about 2 × 225g/ ½ pound jars.

Bergamot, from the mint family, has its own special flavour.

CLEMENTINE AND MINT JELLY

4 clementines
1 small lemon
jam sugar
4 tablespoons medium red wine
pinch of salt
¼ teaspoon white pepper
handful of chopped fresh ginger mint leaves

Peel the rind from the fruit, making sure that no pith adheres. Finely shred and set aside. Chop the pith and flesh and put into a very large bowl with the pips and 200ml/ 7 fl.oz hot water. Cover and cook on Full power for 10 minutes, stirring occasionally to prevent boiling over.
Strain into another similarly sized bowl and stir in the shredded peel. Cover and cook on Full power for 7 minutes or until tender. Measure the volume and add 100g/ 4 ounces sugar to each 150ml/ ¼ pint mixture. Stir in the wine.
Cook for 2 minutes, then stir until the sugar is dissolved. Without covering cook until boiling about 2 minutes, then continue cooking for 5 minutes or until a few drops of the liquid placed on a chilled saucer wrinkles when pushed with a spoon. Stir in the salt, pepper and mint.
Pour into hot sterilized jars and seal in the usual way.

Makes about 350g/ 12 ounces.

The shredded peel adds an interesting texture to this savoury jelly.

GRAPE AND CINNAMON JELLY

450g/ 1 pound sharp green grapes weighed after removing the stalks
jam sugar
¼ teaspoon ground cinnamon

Rinse the grapes and put in a large bowl with 120ml/ 4 fl.oz water. Cover and cook for 8 minutes on Full power, stirring once. Crush with a potato masher. Although the grapes will have collapsed the skins remain tough. Without covering cook on Full power for a further 5 minutes. Crush once more, then drain in a sieve set over another bowl. Press the fruit down to obtain maximum juice. Leave until the mixture ceases to drip and resist the temptation to scrape in the pulp. This process may take about half an hour. About 250ml/ 8 fl.oz juice is extracted but this depends on the size and type of the grapes used.

Measure the juice and add 225g/ 8 ounces sugar for every 250ml/ 8 fl.oz. Stir in the cinnamon. Cover and cook on Full power for 2 minutes, then stir until the sugar is dissolved.

Without covering cook on Full power until boiling, the continue cooking for 4 minutes or until a few drops of the liquid placed on a chilled saucer wrinkle when pushed with a spoon. Strain to remove cinnamon scum and pour into a hot sterilized jar. It is better to have a looser set than continue cooking which will darken this lovely golden jelly.

Makes about 450ml/ 1 pound.

PARSLEY AND MARJORAM JELLY

350g/ 12 ounces cooking apples
50g/ 2 ounces freshly chopped parsley
15g/ ½ ounce fresh marjoram leaves
150ml/ ¼ pint white wine vinegar
jam sugar

Wash and coarsely chop the apples. Put them in a very large bowl with half of the herbs and 150ml/ ¼ pint water. Cover and cook on Full power for 6 minutes or until the apples have pulped. Stir occasionally during cooking for even results. Stir in the vinegar and without covering cook on Full power for 5 minutes or until the mixture reduces slightly. Pour into a nylon sieve lined with muslin or a white J cloth set over a large bowl. Cover and leave to drain for several hours until all the juice has dripped through.

Measure the juice. Return to the bowl and add 100g/ 4 ounces sugar for every 150ml/ ¼ pint juice.

Cover and cook on Full power for 2 minutes, then stir until the sugar is dissolved. Without covering cook on Full power for 6 minutes or until a few drops of the liquid when placed on a chilled saucer wrinkle when pushed with a spoon. Skim the jelly if necessary, then stir in the remaining herbs and cook for a further minute. Leave to cool slightly then stir just before potting to distribute the herbs evenly.

Seal and pot in the usual way.

Makes about 350ml/ 12 fl.oz.

QUINCE AND LEMON BALM JELLY

450g/ 1 pound quinces
1 tablespoon fresh lemon balm leaves
juice of half a lemon
jam sugar

Coarsely chop the quinces and put in a very large bowl with the lemon balm leaves, lemon juice and 200ml/ 7 fl.oz water. Cover and cook on Full power for 10 minutes or until the fruit is soft. Stir frequently during cooking to prevent boiling over.

Strain into another bowl but do not press the pulp through or the jelly will be cloudy. It may be necessary to wait up to 30 minutes for all the juices to drain.

Measure the juice and add 100g/ 4 ounces sugar for every 150ml/ ¼ pint. Cover and cook on Full power for 2 minutes or until hot, then stir until the sugar is dissolved. Without covering continue cooking for 6 minutes or until a few drops of the liquid when placed on a chilled saucer wrinkle when pushed with a spoon.

Leave until cool, then stir to remove any skin that has formed on the surface and pot in the usual way.

Makes about 350g/ 12 ounces.

REDCURRANT JELLY

675g/ 1½ pounds redcurrants
jam sugar

Rinse the redcurrants and pick off any bad fruit. There is no need to remove the stalks. Crush with a potato masher to free some of the juice, then add 150ml/ ¼ pint water. Cover and cook on Full power for 7 minutes or until the colour drains from the fruit.

Crush once more. Line a nylon strainer with muslin or a white J cloth and set over a very large bowl. Cover and leave to strain overnight. Measure the juice and for each 300ml/ ½ pint add 225g/ 8 ounces of sugar. Cover and cook on Full power for 3 minutes, then stir until the sugar is dissolved. Without covering cook on Full power for 2 minutes or until boiling. Continue cooking for 4 minutes or until a few drops of the syrup poured on to a chilled saucer wrinkle when pushed with a spoon.

Pour into a hot sterilized jar and seal in the usual way.

Makes about 300ml/ ½ pint.

CHAPTER EIGHT

Pickles, Chutneys and Relishes

All pickles, chutneys and relishes can be made either entirely or with the help of the microwave oven. My recipes include the two most popular pickle recipes but most conventional recipes can be adapted, the only rule being that only small batches should be attempted.

When making pickles choose only good quality fruit and vegetables, freshly picked if possible and in firm condition. Use distilled white vinegar, malt for preference when it is important to keep the colour bright. A true malt vinegar contains no added colouring and has a high acid content which prevents micro-organisms from spoiling the pickles. Brown malt vinegar, the kind most people have in the larder, is best saved for dark, sweeter pickles or chutneys. Some vinegars sold as malt may have added colouring so look out for the best makes. Cider, wine and speciality vinegars may impart a trace of added flavour but these too will reduce the clarity.

Pickling or coarse granulated salt such as rock salt, do not contain additives. Table salts incorporate anti-caking agents to make them flow freely, eg magnesium carbonate, which does not give such good results.

Chutneys cooked conventionally need long, slow cooking in order to thicken and darken. Since there is a very real danger that the mixture will burn on the bottom, frequent stirring is desirable. Since chutneys contain a large proportion of sugar, in the microwave burning can only occur if the mixture becomes too thick. Occasional stirring is still required to equalise the temperature and prevent thick chutney from bubbling and spattering. Microwave cooking times are dramatically shorter too. Although unlikely, if you do encounter problems with burning, add only half the sugar when directed and mix in the remainder two-thirds of the way through cooking.

Relishes are meant to be consumed soon after preparing as they need no storage time for the flavour to further develop. On the other hand chutneys improve with keeping and must be potted adequately. If jars are not completely airtight the vinegar will evaporate, leaving a hard mass. A little surplus liquid should always be floating on top of the mixture.

90

In common with pickles, any high acid content preserve is liable to 'eat' through metal lids. So it is advisable to place a double thickness waxed disk on top of the mixture before fitting the lid. Some metal lids are coated with non-eroding lacquer but plastic is a far more reliable choice.

BEETROOT AND HORSERADISH RELISH

2 raw beetroot total weight 225g/ 8 ounces
100g/ 4 ounce piece fresh horseradish
50g/ 2 ounces granulated sugar
pinch of salt
150ml/ ¼ pint red wine vinegar

Remove any long stalks and rinse the beetroot if necessary but do not damage the skins. Put into a large bowl with sufficient water to come half-way up the beetroot. Cover with a vented lid or well pierced clingfilm and cook on Full power for 10 minutes or until the beetroot are tender but not soft. Drain and leave to cool.
Peel and grate the beetroot and horseradish. Mix in the sugar, salt and vinegar. Spoon into sterilized screwtop jars and cover with a waxed paper disk before putting on the lid.

Makes about 675g/ 1½ pounds.

GREEN BANANA CHUTNEY

3 under-ripe bananas
6 – 8 spring onions, trimmed
1 small green pepper, cored and de-seeded
6 parsley sprigs
1 tablespoon lemon thyme leaves
1 garlic clove
1 small green chilli, halved and de-seeded
1 tablespoon sultanas
2 tablespoons white wine vinegar
¼ teaspoon ground mace
½ teaspoon salt
2 tablespoons granulated sugar

Whizz all the ingredients in the blender and transfer to a very large bowl.

Cover and cook on Full power for 5 minutes. Stir. Without covering cook on Medium power for 8 minutes or until thick, stirring frequently.

Spoon into a serving dish and leave to cool. The chutney is best served fresh and will darken if kept for more than 24 hours.

Makes 450g/ 1 pound.

LEMON TOMATO CHUTNEY

1 lemon
4 large tomatoes
2 lovage leaves or ½ teaspoon dried lovage
1 tablespoon tomato purée
¼ small onion
pinch chilli powder
6 dates, stoned
¼ teaspoon black peppercorns
¼ teaspoon salt
1 tablespoon medium red wine
50g/ 2 ounces Demerara sugar

Squeeze the juice and pare the rind from the lemon. Place them in the blender with the other ingredients (except the sugar) and whizz briefly to chop.

Pour into a large bowl, cover and cook on Full power for 3 minutes or until boiling. Stir and, without covering, cook for 10 minutes, then mix in the sugar and cook for a further 6 minutes or until thick. Stir occasionally during cooking.

Spoon into a jar and cover with a plastic lid. Refrigerate for 24 hours, then use within a week.

Makes 450g/ 1 pound.

MANGO CHUTNEY

1 under-ripe mango
1cm/ ½ inch piece root ginger
1 clove garlic
25g/ 1 ounce large seedless raisins
50g/ 2 ounces soft brown sugar
3 tablespoons malt vinegar
½ – 1 teaspoon chilli powder (depending on taste)
1 teaspoon English mustard
½ teaspoon salt
1 tablespoon granulated sugar

Peel the mango, then using a sharp, stainless steel knife, slash in a criss-cross fashion on both flatter sides. This is an easier way to dice the fruit than slicing it away from the stone and then chopping. Peel and finely chop the ginger, crush the garlic and finely chop the raisins. Combine all the ingredients except the granulated sugar in a very large bowl. Cover and cook on Full power for 5 minutes. Stir thoroughly, then continue cooking for 5 minutes. Stir and without covering cook on Full power for 5 minutes or until the mixture is thick and only a tablespoon of liquid is visible. Overcooking will result in burning.

Stir in the granulated sugar.

Spoon into a hot sterilized jar and seal with a non-metallic lid or jam pot cover.

Makes 350g/ 12 ounces.

The flavour of the chutney improves after storing for a week or two.

PICCALILLI

75g/ 3 ounces courgette
50g/ 2 ounces green beans
1 celery stalk
175g/ 6 ounces cauliflower florets
75g/ 3 ounces baby onions
salt
1 teaspoon turmeric
2–3 teaspoons mustard powder
25g/ 1 ounce granulated sugar
300ml/ ½ pint distilled white vinegar
½ teaspoon cornflour

Thickly slice the courgette and then cut in half. Slice the beans and celery stalk. Spread all the vegetables out on a plastic tray and generously sprinkle with salt. Cover and leave for 12 hours or overnight.

Thoroughly rinse the vegetables in a colander under cold running water, then drain thoroughly. Put the vegetables, turmeric, mustard, sugar and all but 3 tablespoons of the vinegar in a very large bowl. Stir, then cover and cook on Full power for 4 minutes or until the vegetables are crisp-cooked. Stir until the sugar is dissolved.

Blend the cornflour with the remaining vinegar, pour into the mixture and stir well. Without covering cook on Full power for 2 minutes or until the liquid thickens. Do not overcook as this makes the vegetables too soft.

Leave to cool, then spoon into one or two jars making sure that each is filled to capacity. Press the pickle down with a spoon to remove any air bubbles. Cover with a plastic lid.

Makes about 450g/ 1 pound.

PICKLED RED CABBAGE

1 small red cabbage (weight about 175g/ 6 ounces after trimming)
salt
about 150ml/ ¼ pint white malt vinegar
1 slice ginger root
small piece cinnamon stick
8–10 black peppercorns
pinch chilli powder
4 blades mace
6 cloves
4 whole allspice
1 bay leaf

Discard the outer leaves and thick stem and finely shred the cabbage. Spread out on a non-metallic tray and sprinkle with salt. Cover completely (but not with foil) and leave to stand for 12 hours or overnight.

Pour the vinegar into a bowl or jug and stir in the remaining ingredients. Cook on Full power for 3 minutes or until boiling. Leave to cool.

Rinse and thoroughly drain the cabbage and pack into a jar. Strain the cooled vinegar into the cabbage, making sure that it is completely covered by the liquid. Cover tightly with a plastic lid.

Keep for one week before using. Will keep up to two months, after which the cabbage will soften and lose its bright colour.

Makes about 450g/ 1 pound.

PLOUGHMAN'S CHUTNEY

450g/ 1 pound cooking apples
4 shallots
50g/ 2 ounces stoned dates
50g/ 2 ounces raisins
50g/ 2 ounces dried apricots
½ teaspoon ground ginger
½ teaspoon ground allspice
¼ teaspoon ground cloves
½ teaspoon salt
100g/ 4 ounces Demerara sugar
200ml/ 7 fl.oz malt vinegar

Peel, core and finely chop the apples, finely chop the shallots, dates raisins and apricots. Put into a very large bowl and mix in all the remaining ingredients. Add 3 tablespoons water.
Cover and cook on Full power for 5 minutes. Stir thoroughly, then without covering continue cooking for about 10 minutes or until the mixture is thick. A spoon drawn through the mixture should leave a furrow. Stir frequently during cooking.
Pot in hot sterilized jars and seal with jam pot covers and plastic lids to prevent evaporation.

The chutney is best if kept for a week before use.

Makes 900g/ 2 pounds.

SWEETCORN RELISH

¼ small red pepper, deseeded
25g/ 1 ounce cabbage
1 small onion
225g/ 8 ounces sweetcorn kernels
½ teaspoon turmeric
2 teaspoons French mustard
200ml/ 7 fl.oz white wine vinegar
75g/ 3 ounces granulated sugar
1 teaspoon chopped fresh sage leaves
2 teaspoons flour
½ teaspoon salt

Chop the pepper, cabbage and onion and put into a very large bowl with the sweetcorn and 2 tablespoons water. Cover and cook on Full power for 5 minutes, stirring occasionally.

Add the turmeric, mustard, most of the vinegar, the sugar and sage leaves. Cover and cook on Full power for 10 minutes, stirring occasionally.

Blend the flour, salt and remaining vinegar together and stir into the vegetables.

Without covering cook on Full power for 5 minutes, then stir once more. Reduce the power to Medium and cook for 10 minutes or until the relish is thick but not dry. Stir the mixture from time to time to avoid scorching.

Leave until cold, then spoon into sterilized jar(s) and seal with a plastic lid(s).

Makes about 450g/ 1 pound.

TOMATO AND CAPSICUM CHUTNEY

1 small red pepper
1 small green pepper
1 small yellow pepper
1 large onion
450g/ 1 pound soft ripe tomatoes
50g/ 2 ounces sultanas
75g/ 3 ounces soft dark brown sugar
2 teaspoons salt
1 tablespoon ground ginger
¼ teaspoon paprika
½ teaspoon mustard powder
150ml/ ¼ pint malt vinegar

Remove the core and seeds from the peppers. Cut up the peppers and the onion, then coarsely chop with the tomatoes and sultanas in the food processor or by hand.

Mix all the ingredients in a very large bowl, cover with a vented lid or partially with cling film and cook on Full power for 25 minutes or until the mixture is thick and most of the liquid is absorbed. Be sure to stir every 5 minutes to prevent burning.

Spoon into a clean, dry jar when cool. Cover tightly with a non-metallic lid.

Makes about 450g/ 1 pound.

CHAPTER NINE

Ketchups, Barbecue Sauces and Vinegars

Ketchup conjures up an image of a bottle of red sauce or some indefinable concoction in a squeezy container served in fast food outlets. Granted, bottled tomato ketchup is appetising and of consistent quality, but it also always tastes the same. Home-made ketchup can be equally palate titillating, but much more to the point, its ingredients can be varied with equal success in the microwave.

Historically known as catchup or catsup the modern ketchup is a combination of fruit, vegetables and spices combined to produce a thick pouring sauce. Most ketchups go well with meats and fried fish. They certainly improve the vegetable nut cutlet and even the humble burger can be turned into a special dish when sauced this way. Ketchups can also be used as an extra ingredient to enhance what would otherwise be bland sauces or used as a topping for pizzas.

A ketchup is often composed of ingredients similar to those found in chutneys. The difference is that it is puréed. They keep very well due to their acid content which serves as a preservative. Keep them in bottles or jars with well fitting non-metallic screw top lids.

Barbecue sauces are much like ketchups but may have oil incorporated to aid tenderisation and browning of steaks and chops. Barbecue sauces are useful as marinades as well as the traditional brush on sauce for coating and flavouring the meats as they are cooking on the barbecue.

The role of the microwave in preparing vinegars is mainly one of heating and boiling. The vinegar can be made stronger by cooking on Full or Medium power until well reduced. Vinegar evaporates if heated for long periods, but this is less consequent when prepared by microwave. Tightly lidded with non-metallic caps, vinegars will keep for a very long time.

ELDERBERRY KETCHUP

6 shallots
450g/ 1 pound ripe elderberries
300ml/ ½ pint wine vinegar
1 teaspoon freshly ground black pepper
1 teaspoon ground nutmeg
½ teaspoon ground cloves
1 teaspoon cornflour
1 teaspoon salt

Chop the shallots. Put into a very large bowl with all the other ingredients except the salt and cornflour.

Cover with a vented lid or partially with cling film and cook on Full power for 7 minutes or until the berries are tender.

Reduce the power to Medium, then uncover and cook for 15 minutes. Press the mixture through a nylon sieve into another bowl.

Blend the cornflour with 2 tablespoons water. Add to the purée, stirring thoroughly. Continue cooking on Medium power for 10 minutes, stirring occasionally or until the sauce thickens.

Stir in the salt. Pour into a clean corked bottle.

Makes about 300ml/ ½ pint.

HOT AND PEPPERY BARBECUE SAUCE

1 shallot
2 tablespoons muscovado sugar
150ml/¼ pint bottled tomato ketchup
175ml/ 6 fl.oz cider vinegar
2 tablespoons Worcestershire sauce
1–2 teaspoons chilli powder

Very finely chop the shallot and set aside.
Put the sugar in a large bowl and stir in 150ml/ ¼ pint boiling water.
Stir until the sugar is dissolved. If you wish to speed things up cook
on Full power for 2 minutes, then stir again.
Add the ketchup, vinegar, Worcestershire sauce, chilli powder and
the chopped shallot. Stir well, then cook on Full power for 15
minutes or until reduced by one-third. Stir frequently during
cooking.
Leave until cool, then spoon into a clean jar fitted with a plastic
screw top lid. Use cold prior to barbecuing.

Makes about 300ml/ ½ pint.

This sauce goes well with red meats.

IMPROMPTU BARBECUE SAUCE

1 large onion
1 tablespoon vegetable oil
3 tablespoons tomato purée
3 tablespoons bottled sweet pickle
1 tablespoon lemon juice
¼ teaspoon mustard powder

Very finely chop the onion and put into a very large bowl with the oil. Mix thoroughly and cook on Full power for 5 minutes or until the onion starts to brown. Stir occasionally to ensure even cooking. Add the remaining ingredients and 200ml/ 7 fl.oz hot water. Cook on Full power for 10 minutes or until the onion is soft.

Purée in the blender, then if necessary return to the bowl and continue cooking until reduced to a thin pouring consistency.

Use as a basting sauce or serve separately. This sauce goes very well with lamb.

Makes about 300ml/ ½ pint.

LEMON AND ORANGE ENHANCER SAUCE

1 lemon
1 orange
2 shallots
1 cm/ ½ inch slice fresh horseradish
3 anchovy fillets, well drained
1 teaspoon salt
¼ teaspoon ground mace
¼ teaspoon ground cloves
¼ teaspoon ground ginger
pinch of chilli powder
25g/ 1 ounce granulated sugar
1 tablespoon tomato purée
150ml/ ¼ pint red wine vinegar

Grate the lemon and orange rind, remove the pith and pips and chop the flesh. Finely chop the shallots, horseradish and anchovies. Put all the ingredients in a large bowl.

Cover and cook on Full power for 2 minutes or until boiling. Stir well, then uncover and cook on Full power for 10 minutes or until reduced by one-third. Stir occasionally during cooking.

Cover and leave until cold, then strain into a jug and pour into a bottle fitted with a cork or plastic lid.

Makes about 175ml/ 6 fl.oz.

LEMON VERBENA MARINADE

1 tablespoon fresh or 1 teaspoon dried lemon verbena leaves
150ml/ ¼ pint medium red wine
2 tablespoons chicken stock
1 small onion
2 tablespoons olive oil
½ teaspoon salt
¼ teaspoon freshly ground black pepper

Put the lemon verbena leaves, wine and stock in a large bowl. Finely slice the onion and add to the mixture. Cover and cook on Full power for 3 minutes or until boiling.
Leave until cold, then stir in the oil, salt and pepper. Use as required. Can be stored in the freezer but this will discolour the lemon verbena leaves.

Makes 200ml/ 7 fl.oz.

NATURAL TOMATO KETCHUP

900g/ 2 pounds ripe tomatoes
2 medium onions
1 red pepper
1 clove garlic
250ml/ 8 fl.oz red wine vinegar
100g/ 4 ounces dark soft brown sugar
½ teaspoon salt
¼ teaspoon freshly ground black pepper
½ cinnamon stick
3 bay leaves
½ teaspoon celery seeds
1 teaspoon mustard seeds
1 small red chilli

Coarsely cut up the tomatoes, thinly slice the onions and core, deseed and slice the red pepper. Crush the garlic. Put these ingredients and the vinegar in a very large bowl. Cover and cook on Full power for about 6 minutes or until the vegetables are soft, stirring occasionally. Purée, if necessary in batches, in the blender, then press through a sieve into another bowl. Stir in all the remaining ingredients.

Cover and cook on Full power until boiling (about 3 minutes). Uncover and continue cooking for 10 minutes or until the mixture thickens to tomato ketchup consistency. Stir occasionally during cooking to prevent splattering.

Strain once more to remove all seeds, the cinnamon stick and bay leaves. Cover and leave until cold.

Pour into bottles or jars and seal with non-metallic lids.

Makes about 600ml/ 1 pint.

RASPBERRY VINEGAR

100g/ 4 ounces raspberries
300ml/ ½ pint red wine vinegar
pinch of salt
50g/ 2 ounces granulated sugar

Put the raspberries, vinegar and salt into a screw top jar fitted with a plastic lid. Make sure the vinegar covers the fruit. Leave for 3–4 days, gently shaking the jar each day. Without putting pressure on the raspberries, strain the vinegar into a large bowl.

Stir in the sugar and cook on Full power for 2 minutes. Stir until the sugar is dissolved, then continue cooking for 4 minutes or until boiling. Reduce the power and cook on Medium for 10 minutes.

Cover and leave until cold, then pour into the jar or half-size wine bottle. Cover with a plastic lid or cork and store for 3 weeks before using to develop the flavour.
Keeps well.

Makes 300ml/ ½ pint.

SPICED VINEGAR

4 whole allspice
8 green peppercorns
2 juniper berries
4 cloves
1cm/ ½ inch piece cinnamon stick
300ml/ ½ pint malt vinegar

Put the allspice, peppercorns and juniper berries on a piece of greaseproof paper. Fold the paper to enclose them, then punch with the head of a rolling pin to bruise but not crush the berries. Tip them into a very large bowl and add all the other ingredients.
Cook on Full power for 3 minutes or until boiling. Stir to mix the hotter with the cooler parts, then continue cooking until the vinegar comes back to the boil.
Using oven gloves remove the bowl from the microwave, cover tightly and leave for 3 or more hours to allow the spices to infuse. Strain and pour into a corked bottle.

Makes 300ml/ ½ pint.

VICTORIA CATCHUP

700g / 1½ pounds under-ripe Victoria plums
1 small Bramley cooking apple
350g / 12 ounces Demerara sugar
150ml / ¼ pint white malt vinegar
pinch of cinnamon
pinch of salt
½ teaspoon juniper berries, crushed to a powder

Rinse the plums, peel, core and coarsely chop the apple, then put the fruit in a very large bowl with 3 tablespoons water. Cover and cook on Full power for 10 minutes or until the fruit is soft.
Stir occasionally to prevent overspill.
Press through a sieve to remove the stones and stalks if any. Return the resulting purée to the bowl. Stir in the sugar, cover and cook on Full power for 3 minutes or until dissolved, then add the remaining ingredients. Without covering cook on Full power for 15 minutes or until the ketchup is of a thick pouring consistency.
Pour into hot sterilized jars or ketchup bottles and seal in the usual way.
If you decide to re-use a bottle, cover the mouth of the bottle with a disc of Porosan skin before screwing on the lid.

Makes about 600ml/ 1 pint.

The initial cooking time can be reduced by chopping the apples more finely but little time will be saved because preparation time is inevitably increased.

Index of Recipes